The Young Rider

The Young Rider

Robert Owen
&
John Bullock

COUNTRY LIFE BOOKS

by the same authors

Robert Owen
My Learn to Ride Book
Successful Riding and Jumping

John Bullock
The Horse and Pony Quiz Book

Robert Owen and John Bullock
The Horse and Pony Gift Book
Buying and Keeping a Horse or Pony
Caring for a Horse or Pony
Riding and Schooling
About Jumping

Published by Country Life Books
and distributed for them by
The Hamlyn Publishing Group Limited
London · New York · Sydney · Toronto
Astronaut House, Feltham, Middlesex, England

First published 1977
Second impression 1978

ISBN 0 600 39527 8

Printed in Italy by
New Interlitho Limited, Milan

Contents

List of Illustrations

The authors acknowledge the help they have received from: The Bookham Riding Centre, Surrey; Francesca and Sally Bullock; Ann Commins; Mr. John Elliot; Mrs. Liz Ferrand; Grange Farm, Stoke Poges, Buckinghamshire; Mr. and Mrs. Ian Grant; Susan Grant; Mr. and Mrs. Ronald Hancock; Anne-Marie and Richard Hancock; Mr. John Howard; Mr. and Mrs. Gerry Howe; Andrew and Katie Howe; Mr. Leslie Lane; Keith Luxford (Saddlery) Limited; Alison Owen; Mr. A. R. H. Thomas; Mr. and Mrs. Charles Thompson; Hilary and Carolyn Thompson.

Introduction

The Young Rider has been written and designed for all who love horses and ponies and, although primarily intended for the younger person, the book should be of interest to the many adults who are now being drawn into the saddle for the first time. Riding is an activity enjoyed by millions throughout the world, but the maximum amount of true pleasure comes as the rider increases his knowledge of the many aspects of equitation.

Among the first things he will learn, and everyone will go through their riding life learning something new each day, is how to care and look after a horse or pony. By this we do not mean simply seeing he is well fed and watered. That part of caring for an animal is, of course, most important. But there is so much more!

There is the need for daily attention and grooming, and the understanding of the importance of hygiene and cleanliness. A good rider will know how to check a horse's well-being and general health. He will also know why it is essential to be firm but kind and considerate at all times.

The Young Rider deals with that side of equitation, just as it deals with riding and improving riding knowledge. In the pages about riding we discuss the action of the horse, and the movement from one pace to another. We look at exercising and the questions which continually are being asked about saddlery and equipment. We also examine training methods to ensure the improvement of both horse and rider.

The best way of learning to ride is by taking lessons from qualified or competent instructors, for only at such lessons can bad habits be explained and corrected, and any errors quickly put right. The purposes of this book are to compliment riding instruction, to give guidance to those who wish to understand more about horsemanship, and to offer a useful book of reference.

For those who have yet to start riding, or who are taking riding lessons, and for those who are already competent in the saddle, we hope there will be much here to encourage still better riding and a wider understanding of the horse. After all, these must be the objectives we are setting out to achieve.

1
Buying a horse or pony

The purchase of a horse or pony requires considerable care and thought because whatever the type of animal being bought there are always the unknown problems of temperament, soundness, suitability and ability.

The more experience you have the easier it is to minimise these risks, but always keep in mind that no two animals are really alike. One which may seem very near to perfection when you try him at his owner's premises may prove to be just the reverse when you get him home. Finding the right horse or pony calls for patience, careful searching, sensible vetting and, preferably, a thorough trial.

Before setting out to find the right animal, make sure that you really have a clear picture of what you want. Apart from knowing the height, age, class and shape of the pony you would like, it is also important to have some idea of temperament, ability and price, bearing in mind where the animal is going to be kept.

Thoroughbreds do not usually do well out at grass all the year round, but neither do mountain and moorland ponies enjoy the continuous confines of a stable. Mountains and moorlands are usually much happier when they are free to roam about in conditions more in keeping with their natural surroundings.

The first essential decision you will have to make is the type, age and size of animal. If other people are providing the money do try and persuade them not to make the mistake of buying a horse or pony which is far too big, merely because they think that you will 'grow into it'. That would be wrong. Everyone needs a horse or pony they can manage safely by themselves. They do not want to be carted about by an animal which is far too large for them.

Ponies in particular require a certain amount of discipline and in the case of a juvenile rider the chances are that by the time they are old enough to ride it properly the pony will have become spoilt and nearly unmanageable. It is also a mistake for parents to buy a pony which is too young in the expectation that their son or daughter and the pony will grow up together. An older pony will prove much more satisfactory, unless there is someone available with the knowledge, ability and time neces-

sary regularly to school the pony. Even then the young rider would probably have more fun and also learn more from a pony which is reliable and sensible enough to be ridden and looked after without the need for constant supervision.

Some riders of fourteen and fifteen years of age are already too big for a pony, and need a horse. It is wrong to be under-horsed or over-horsed, and the choice of animal should depend on your own ability and ambitions, along with that ever present problem – the amount of money you can afford to pay.

First pony

Ponies fall into various categories, and are usually advertised under different headings describing the type of activity to which they are best suited. A child's first pony should be one which is entirely reliable, and has the necessary experience, manners and temperament to instil confidence in a young novice rider. It will be traffic-proof – and possibly getting on in age. The latter will not matter so much because the pony will probably have been bought because of temperament and manners.

Grand Duke, a magnificent two-year-old Arab colt

14

A specially posed photograph showing, *left,* a rider who is far too big for the pony and, *right,* a young man who is much too small to be comfortable on the horse.

Child's second pony

A child's second pony should still be an animal which can be controlled at all paces by a relatively inexperienced rider, and will be free of vices. It will, however, be schooled to a stage where its rider can learn more advanced movements.

Child's hunter

If the pony is referred to as a child's hunter it should be a good jumper and capable of carrying his rider across country. It may not be a particularly beautiful pony, but it will be well mannered, and make up with ability anything it may lack in looks.

Show pony

A child's show pony is usually of the miniature thoroughbred type, with a price tag to match its elegance and looks. The more successful these ponies have been, the higher will be their price. They will be costed according to their training, conformation, action and temperament in the show ring. Height is also important because Show Classes carry height limitations.

Gymkhana pony

Gymkhana classes are tremendously popular at local shows in Britain and a great deal of fun can be had with a good fast and handy gymkhana pony which is steady enough in temperament to stand when required, and will also put up with the noise, jostling, shouting and general disturbance of gymkhana events. They are useful in introducing a young rider to competitions and the show ring. Many fine riders started by winning gymkhana races.

Family pony

A type of pony which is very much underestimated is the General

Utility or Family pony. He is the type who will carry almost any member of the family. Although he may not excel at anything in particular, he will be willing to have a go at everything—from pulling a dog cart to taking an elder brother or sister out hunting. Looks will be of secondary importance. Sturdiness, gameness and temperament will give him the edge over some of his more fancy companions.

Leading Rein classes are the first opportunity most young riders have for gaining experience in the Show ring

Show jumper or eventer

The increased popularity of Show Jumping and Eventing in many countries has brought to the fore the child's show jumper and Eventer. Although show jumpers are usually judged only on their ability to jump big courses against the clock, and age, conformation, and schooling are of secondary importance, the same is not true of the young rider's Eventer. This type of horse or pony must be able to carry out a good dressage test; be bold and clever enough to tackle a long, complicated and often quite demanding cross country course, and then do a faultless show jumping round.

Unlike the young rider's show jumper, he will not necessarily have to be of any particular height because Events are not judged on height.

Most pony show jumping classes go up in hands—from 12 hands 2 inches to 13·2 and finally 14·2. In Britain, for example,

The start of a gymkhana event

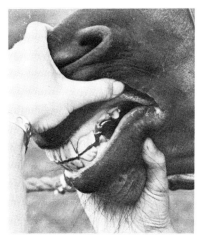

Age is checked by examination of the teeth

the best show jumping ponies are registered with the British Show Jumping Association according to their size and are graded according to the amount of prize money they have won. One advantage of buying a Registered pony is that the Association will provide accurate details of how successful it has been, and also give some guide as to the animal's past history. It is, however, as well to remember that, like their larger counterparts, show jumping ponies do get over-jumped and they can then become stale.

Whatever the pony or horse being purchased, it is very important to have the animal carefully vetted. A trial at home may not always be possible, but if the owner is really anxious to ensure the right sort of new home a trial can often be arranged providing you take out suitable insurance cover.

Having decided on the type, height and age of animal you require, the search should start. There is an old saying 'buy in haste and repent at leisure'. While that is certainly true, there are various safe ways of trying to find the right animal. It is, for example, best to buy from somebody you know personally. The history of the animal can then be verified – and the good and bad points should become evident. The opinions of people who have seen the horse or pony perform can be sought but, even so, it is always wise to have the final advice of a veterinary surgeon.

17

Some Riding Schools buy and sell horses and ponies. Although they are obviously in business to make money, the reputable establishments go to considerable lengths to guard their good names, to make sure that the animals they are selling are suitable for the work the purchaser requires them to do. They will also often be willing to exchange a horse or pony if it does not come up to the expectations of the purchaser.

The majority of horses and ponies are sold through Sale Yards and Auctions, and if the 'warranty' scheme is in force it safeguards the purchaser to a considerable extent. Even so, the Auction ring is no place for the novice as purchases made there must naturally be something of a gamble. There are, of course, bargains to be had, but owners of good horses and ponies like

to know where they are going – and sell them privately.

Replying to an advertisement in a local paper or specialised horse magazine is one way of finding the right animal. However, a wiser way is to advertise yourself for *exactly* what is required. Ask for a photograph in addition to full details as to height, age, performance, soundness and price, and start by seeing the likely animals first which are nearest home.

If you have limited experience of horse dealing, try and take someone with you who understands it. Always ask to see the potential horse or pony being ridden by someone else before getting into the saddle yourself. If it rears, bucks or bolts it is better to know what to expect before finding yourself on the receiving end of trouble.

2

Popular breeds

There are more than one hundred recognised breeds and types of horses and ponies in the world. Although the Thoroughbred has had a great deal of influence in the development of many breeds, some countries are famous for their own special types of horse or pony, which have been produced over the years for a particular purpose.

British Thoroughbreds trace back to the time of Charles II, who was passionately fond of horse-racing and did much to encourage the sport. The history of the Thoroughbred goes back nearly as far in the United States of America.

The better a horse's breeding, the more likely are his characteristics to be fixed in him and be passed on to his descendants.

Both the stallion and the mare can stamp their own type and make-up on their off-spring and so a foal will usually be a blend of its parents' qualities and defects. If one of the parents is the better bred, however, then that parent's qualities will be predominant. For this reason the British Thoroughbred has been used extensively over the years to improve many native breeds.

The potency of the Arab in this respect is probably even greater – and his blood permeates that of the Thoroughbred himself. One great quality of the Arab is that he is much less liable to develop the many hereditary unsoundnesses that are such a problem in other breeds – including those of the bone and the wind.

However valuable the Thoroughbred and the Arab blood may be in helping to improve native breeds, there must be a reasonable affinity between the types to be crossed.

Temperament, conformation, constitution, colour and soundness are all-important, and for this reason many of the mountain and moorland breeds of Britain have earned very high reputations as ideal mounts for young riders.

BRITISH NATIVE PONY BREEDS
Highland
The largest and strongest of the mountain and moorland breeds is the Highland pony from Scotland. The Mainland is the larger of the Highland breeds. There is also a smaller type known as

Right, top: Highland
centre: Fell
bottom: Dales

the Western Islands pony, bred in the Hebrides.

Highland ponies vary in height from 12·2 to 14·2 hands and are usually grey or dun-coloured, although there are sometimes browns and blacks. Occasionally some of the ponies bred in the Western Isles are chestnut and have silver manes and tails.

The Highland breed of pony has stocky, powerful limbs, short back and attractive head with very intelligent eyes. Although they do not accept strangers quickly, they have kind temperaments and are in great demand by trekkers wanting to ride across the beautiful Scottish countryside.

Fell

The Pennine range of mountains down the centre of Britain separates the famous Dales ponies from the Fell ponies (from whom they descend). Fell and Dales ponies used to be the same breed, differing only by the places where they were raised.

Fell ponies standing between 13 and 14 hands in height, were bred originally as pack-animals for carrying heavy loads of lead in panniers slung on either side of their backs from the mines to the docks. For this task they needed good shoulders, muscular quarters and strong legs and clean joints. Their hooves became hard, with a rather characteristic blue horn.

21

Left and above: Handsome and well-bred

For a long time Fell ponies were also used in coal mines and to sledge peat from the hills down into the valleys.

They are still in frequent use for shepherding and light harness work and, being extremely hardy, they can live out all the year round and withstand really cold weather. With their long necks and handsome heads they make very useful and attractive children's ponies.

Dales

The Dales ponies were also used for carrying lead to the docks, but being rather stronger than the Fell they were, in addition, used for farm work.

Their greater strength came from being crossed with heavier breeds—with Clydesdales in particular. So much so that they lost much of the pony-like characteristics and have now developed into 'small horses' up to a considerable amount of weight.

They stand about 14·2 hands high and are really good dual purpose ponies, being able to work in harness and are also agile enough to carry a man riding or even hunting.

In their natural surroundings they seem to survive well on rough grazing, and are rarely turned out to run on the moors. Their neat heads with small ears, and their short necks well placed on strong compact bodies with sturdy legs make them very attractive little 'horses'. Although they are mostly black or brown in colour, there are some greys and bays–but never chestnuts, skewbalds or piebalds.

Shetland

Further north the Shetland pony is the smallest and perhaps the best known of all pony breeds. Some breeders would claim that it is a descendant of the little Plains horses of Central America. The rough climate and sparse diet of the Shetland Isles has undoubtedly been partly responsible for their small size.

They are remarkably strong, have been known to carry a full grown man up to 40 miles in a day, and have also travelled long distances as pack ponies.

They are docile and lovable, though inclined to be strong willed. Because they are so small, they are often used to introduce very young children to riding. Indeed, because of their size, they are frequently measured in inches instead of hands–42 inches is the limit allowed for a pony if it is to be registered in the *Shetland Pony Stud Book*.

Apart from their size, Shetlands are easily recognizable by their small heads and muzzles, neat short ears, large kind eyes,

Above: Dartmoor

Connemara

24

compact bodies, short sturdy legs and very long thick manes and tails.

Connemara

The Irish have always been famed as natural horsemen, and they also show great skill in breeding fine horses and ponies. The Connemara, with its Spanish influence has, over the years, become well known as an excellent family pony in countries many thousands of miles away from its native area of Connaught.

In Ireland the Connemara ponies frequently have to live out on rough hillsides, with little food or protection. They also need to be sure-footed enough to negotiate the boulders and loose rocks of the mountain slopes. Added to this and their native stamina, they also possess the cunning needed to avoid the quagmires and bogs of the valleys. There is really little wonder that the Connemara ponies have become world-famous for their sturdiness, reliability, and adaptability.

The Connemara Pony Breeders Society, founded in 1923, will only fully register ponies after they have reached the age of three. This ensures that they are between 13·0 and 14·2 hands high and show the necessary good conformation, with plenty of bone and character.

Dartmoor

Although the Dartmoor, from the west of England, has now developed into an easily recognisable breed, it is really the result of cross-breeding over the years with a number of other breeds— including the Arab. They make fine show ponies with their small, neat heads and alert ears, strong, well-muscled backs and

New Forest

25

Above: a small rider needs a small pony like this Shetland

Left: a Welsh cob mare and foal

good, tough legs with evenly shaped feet.

Their low, free action and elegant conformation seem to be emphasised by full and wavy tails set high on their rumps. Dartmoor ponies should not exceed 12·2 hands in height. Their temperament and good looks also make them popular children's ponies.

Dartmoor is similar, in many ways, to the Fell country. It has large areas of unbroken and uncultivated grassland and scrub with sporadic clumps of bracken. Despite their thick coats Dartmoor ponies can suffer from the cold. They do need plenty of good and adequate shelter in really cold weather.

New Forest

The New Forest pony from the South of England is probably one of the most interesting of the British breeds because it has a completely different blood-line from the other native ponies – the result of its very mixed background.

Stretching over nearly 50,000 acres of open moorland, interspersed with roads, the New Forest provides a challenge to the survival of these clever, nimble footed ponies. In bad weather they have to forage hard for their food, but in the warm summer months the thousands of sightseers and holidaymakers using the network of roads through the New Forest are a hazard.

Although many of the roads are now fenced, and there are

Right: Welsh ponies—Section B

Left: Welsh cob

Exmoor

penalties for motorists who stop to feed the ponies, the New Forest is such a docile and friendly animal that many people cannot resist the temptation to stop their cars and entice them down onto the roadways. The ponies look well bred, with their nice, free action. They are also sure footed and their lack of fear with traffic makes them particularly good for children. Their smart appearance and good action also make them popular in harness.

Most New Forest ponies stand about 14·2 hands high and are bright bay, black or brown in colour. The only firm rule regarding colour, however, is that they should never be piebald or skewbald.

Exmoor

Probably the oldest breed of pony in Britain is the Exmoor, thought to date back to pre-Roman times. Like the Welsh they have had to survive the rampages of man. In times of war they have been eaten for food, but King Henry VIII probably wrought most havoc among the pony breeds when he ordered that all horses under 15 hands in height were to be destroyed. Luckily some ponies, such as the Exmoor, living in the more isolated areas of Britain, escaped this death penalty with the result that the breed is still flourishing.

Exmoor ponies are ideal for children. They are keen jumpers, and are easy to keep as they are quite happy living out all the year round. They also possess considerable strength and endurance and frequently live to a great age. Add to these qualities their good temperaments and friendly dispositions, and they can provide any keen young rider with the opportunity successfully to take part in all types of riding activity from hacking and hunting to show jumping and eventing.

Exmoors have their own distinctive colouring – which is

usually brown, bay or dun with mealy-coloured nostrils. The texture of their coats is also different from other native breeds, being stringy and harsh in winter and hard and shiny in summer. The underside of their tummies is also frequently mealy in colour, particularly during the winter months.

Exmoor ponies, usually standing about 12·2 hands high, have deep wide chests, good shoulders, clean, short legs and small, hard feet. Their heads are rather on the long side with a deep set jaw, short, thick ears, mealy-coloured inside, and large eyes set in a broad forehead.

Welsh

Welsh ponies and cobs are hardy and full of quality, making them excellent mounts for young riders. The Welsh Pony and Cob Society places great emphasis on the need for ponies and cobs to work, instead of being bred purely for showing. There are three distinct breeds—the Welsh Mountain Pony, the Welsh Pony, and the Welsh Cob.

The Welsh Mountain pony is perhaps the prettiest and, at the time of writing, the most popular of the nine breeds which form the Mountain and Moorland group. These attractive little ponies have lived in the mountains of Wales for more than a thousand years and, like the Exmoor, suffered less than other breeds during the reign of Henry VIII.

The hardships they have had to endure made them develop a hardiness and intelligence which has made them famous as one of the best foundations for horse and pony breeding in the world.

A Welsh mountain pony is smaller than the Welsh pony. Most are about 12 hands high. Their little, attractive heads with their bold eyes, and small, pointed ears, should be well set on the neck, and their muzzles tapered and soft to the touch. The neck must not be too short, the shoulders long and sloping. The tail carriage is important with the tail set high on the mountain pony's strong, short back, and its action should be free, quick and straight.

The Welsh pony is a real ride and drive pony, and its breeding is a combination of the Mountain Pony and the Cob. It is an animal full of quality with plenty of bone and a hardy constitution, making it an ideal second pony. The Welsh may be up to 13·2 hands in height. This increase in size was achieved by the introduction of Thoroughbred, Hackney and Arab blood some years ago.

These ponies have been used for generations as general purpose animals by Welsh hill farmers, who have employed them for herding sheep and cattle and for rounding up wild mountain ponies. They have been used for hunting over rough and often mountainous ground, showing speed and agility and the balance needed to gallop up and downhill without stumbling.

The origin of the Welsh Cob is not known but it was well established as a breed in the fifteenth century when references

Quarter horse

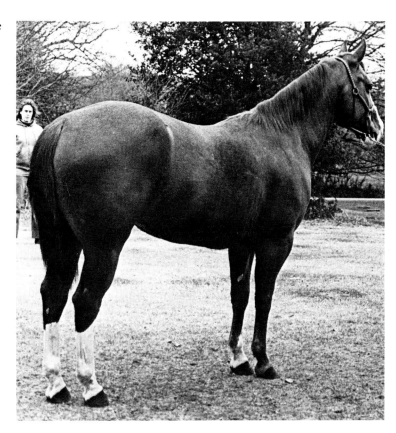

were made to the Cob's ability to 'carry weight, gallop, jump and swim'.

Of the two main Cob breeding areas, Cardiganshire and Pembrokeshire became the home of the larger Cobs, while the smaller cobs, with their greater pony characteristics, were bred in the more mountainous areas of Breckonshire and Radnorshire.

Welsh cobs must be more than 13·2 hands in height and be strong, hardy and active with as much substance as possible. Heads should be full of quality with bold prominent eyes and neat well-set ears. They must have plenty of bone 'below the knee' to make them good, sturdy weight-carriers.

The true action of a Welsh Cob is free and forceful in character, with the whole of the foreleg extended straight from the shoulder, and as far forward as possible during the trot.

OTHER BREEDS
Quarter Horse

The American Quarter Horse is one of the oldest breeds in the United States of America and traces its ancestry to the horses taken to America from Britain in the seventeenth and early eighteenth centuries. It gets its name for its speed in quarter-mile races which used to be a favourite distance with early settlers. The Quarter Horse is sometimes known as the 'cutting horse' because it is used by cowboys for 'cutting out' individual cattle from herds. A short, muscular type of animal, the Quarter Horse stands about 15·2 hands high, and is considered to be descended from the Spanish horses which found their way into America hundreds of years ago.

Morgan

The Morgan was once the most famous of all American horses. Although at one time it was also the most popular numerically, some time ago the United States Government had to take action to make sure that the strain did not die out.

Standing not more than 15 hands high, the Morgan is said to have both Thoroughbred and Arab blood in its veins. It is named after the founder of the breed, Justin Morgan, who called the original sire after himself.

Saddle Horse

The American Saddle Horse is the type now in most common use in the United States of America for hacking, hunting and jumping. The breed originated in the pioneering days four centuries ago when there were no indigenous breeds, and the settlers brought imported breeds from many parts of the world – including the Thoroughbreds.

The breed, which averages 15·0 to 15·3 hands in height, exhibits considerable brilliance and good breeding, and has a particularly distinguishable high head and tail carriage. Bay, brown and chestnut are the most popular colours.

Apart from the usual paces, some saddle horses have two additional gaits. There is a slow gait, and rack which is a single-footed pace in which each foot comes down singly but with considerable speed. The three-gaited Saddle Horses often have clipped manes and tails, whereas the five-gaited horses have full manes and tails.

Appaloosa

Chinese paintings of 3,000 years ago show spotted horses, and they have been known over the years in many parts of the world. The most famous of all the spotted horses is probably the American Appaloosa, whose name is derived from a breed which was developed by the Nez Percé Indians in the Palouse country of Idaho. A similar type is the Colorado Ranger.

Appaloosas are recognised by their pink skins and silky, white coats with their large numbers of spots of varying sizes which can be seen mainly on the quarters. The spots are usually black or brown in colour, but some Appaloosas have white spots on a darker coat. The three usual types of marking are known as leopard, blanket and snowflake, and the breed is noted for its excellent temperament and great qualities of endurance.

Knabstrup, Pinzgauer and Blagden

It is wrong to refer to all spotted horses as Appaloosas. There are other quite definite breeds which have spots as a characteristic or in which spots are likely to occur – such as the Danish Knab-

A Hackney in harness

strup and the Austrian Pinzgauer. Some years ago there was also the Blagden, a spotted horse from Wales.

Hackney

The Hackney, as we know it today, was evolved about the same time as the Thoroughbred racehorse by the use of oriental stallions with native mares whose natural gait was trotting. In Britain the counties where hackneys or trotting horses predominated were Yorkshire, Lincolnshire and Norfolk.

The Hackney Horse Society was formed in 1884 under the patronage of His Royal Highness the Prince of Wales, who, a little later, founded a Hackney stud at Wolverton. As a result, wealthy people throughout Britain took to breeding and showing Hackney horses and ponies. They became enthused by the high-stepping action and characteristic gait.

There was at that time a big demand for high-stepping carriage horses, not only in Britain but also from cities like Paris and Brussels, and indeed from nearly all the capitals of the world. In the 1890's, breeders started to send Hackneys to the United States of America. The Hackney soon asserted his superiority in the show rings and his popularity grew on both sides of the Atlantic. The height of a Hackney varies between 14·3 and 15·3 hands, but some reach 16·2 hands.

The Hackney Horse Society was formed in 1884 to promote and encourage the breeding of general utility horses, harness horses, hackneys, cobs and ponies.

Hackney Pony

The Hackney Pony is a smaller edition of the Hackney Horse with his long neck, good shoulders, compact body and hard limbs. Most Hackneys are bay, brown and black in colour and although there are some chestnut horses there are few chestnut ponies.

Hanoverian

In many parts of Europe, horse breeding has developed into a major industry. The German Hanoverian horses became famous throughout the world because of their show jumping successes. Originally the Hanoverian was much heavier than he is today, and was used for drawing coaches and ploughs in times of peace and guns in time of war. The introduction of Thoroughbred blood, however, has resulted in a much smarter and lighter framed type of saddle horse. The breed owes much to the Hanoverian Kings, who from the time of George I to 1837 sent many Thoroughbreds to Germany to improve the quality while still insisting on the breed maintaining plenty of bone.

Haflinger

The Haflinger is a small, mountain pack pony mostly found in Bavaria and the Tyrol. They are sure-footed and able to carry heavy loads without difficulty. Haflingers are mostly chestnut in colour with pale cream or yellow manes and tails, and are believed to be descended from the Noriker pack pony which can be traced back to the ancient Roman province of Noricum where the pony got its name.

About 14 hands in height, the Haflingers are thick-set—showing great strength and plenty of bone. They carry their heads close to the ground when climbing and this is particularly noticeable when they are being used in agricultural and forestry work.

Polish Arabs

Poland is another country where horses play an important part

Haflinger

in the economy. Each year thousands of them are bred on private farms – and at Government studs – for riding and driving. All pure bred horses have to be registered in the stud book kept by each particular area of the country, and every region breeds its own particular type of horse.

Arabs have been bred in Poland for more than three hundred years, and Polish Arabs have been sold in many parts of the world. The Polish Arab Stud has been developed to ensure that only the true desert type of animal, with the right sort of temperament, is used for breeding.

Camargue
The Camargue area in the South of France has become well known for its white horses, featured in many films and made famous by sculptors and artists. The tough and agile Camargue pony is used to herd the fierce black bulls of the Carmargue, often referred to as the 'Cowboy Country of France'.

The native Normandy breeds were once noted as carriage horses, but the Thoroughbred influence has become more pronounced and now horses from that area are better known for riding and as brilliant show jumpers.

Percheron
France is of course famous for its draught horses like the Percheron and hundreds of them are still exported and used in farming areas where a large, strong, intelligent horse is of far more use than a machine.

Andalusian and Lipizzaner
The very beautiful Andalusian horses in Spain have had a considerable influence on horse breeding in many other countries. The Lipizzaner horses of the Spanish Riding School in Vienna

are, of course, world famous. It is known as the Spanish School because the horses used there are direct descendants of the horses of Andalusia in Spain.

A rather different type of horse is to be found in Australia, where racing the Australian Thoroughbred is a passion which has developed into quite a flourishing industry. Most of the Australian Thoroughbreds can be traced to horses taken to Australia from Britain.

Waler

The native breed of the country, however, is the Australian Waler or Australian Stockhorse which is the result of horses imported from South Africa by the early settlers and crossed with Thoroughbreds. Although only about 15 hands high, the Waler is an excellent, natural jumper and the obvious choice of the Australian cowboy because of his speed and long stride which enables him to cover many miles of country each day without undue stress or strain. The name 'Waler' is an abbreviation of New South Wales where the horse was originally bred.

Brumby

The Brumby is the wild horse of Australia descended from saddle horses which have strayed from the Ranches and Cattle Stations and never been rounded up. With 'paddocks' of 10,000 acres or more it is easy to understand how strays can remain loose for long periods without being caught. Very few of these horses ever become of much use for riding or other work – even when they are caught – because of their wild natures. On Australian racecourses a wild and uncontrollable horse is sometimes referred to as a 'Brumbie'.

Top: Fjord ponies
Centre: Lipizzaner
Above: Waler

Left: Percherons

3

Stable management

There are traditionally four ways of keeping a horse or pony. If you have the necessary facilities at home or nearby you can look after him yourself or with the help of the family—or perhaps there may be a groom to look after him for you. If not you will have to keep him at livery at a Riding Stable, where you will pay a weekly charge for his upkeep. You will, of course, also have to pay the blacksmith and any veterinary bills. He will be exercised for you—and you will be able to ride him as and when you wish to do so. Some stables can be persuaded to keep ponies at half-livery. This means that the owners of the stables have the use of the pony themselves for riding lessons or hacking during certain times of the week, and the livery charge is reduced accordingly.

Looking after the animal yourself is naturally the most satisfying way of being a horse-owner, but you must be prepared for plenty of hard work over long hours. If you enjoy lying in bed in the morning, then think twice before becoming an owner-rider. You might be better off going to the local stables and riding a horse that somebody else has got ready for you. But if you do you will miss the pleasure and satisfaction of looking after your own horse and developing that bond of friendship and trust which only horse-owners, who have cared for their own animals, can really appreciate.

Keeping and looking after a horse must be a labour of love. He will have to be fed and watered regularly and looked after properly. If he becomes ill you may well have to put his needs before your own.

You may have bought a pony which can be kept out all the year round. Even so there will be times when you will want to bring him into a stable, and need to know how to look after him while he is there.

Unless you are fortunate enough to have a suitable stable yard and loose boxes already available, you will either have to convert an existing building into a stable, build one of your own, or perhaps buy a new one. There are usually a number of reputable firms who supply prefabricated stables that only need to be assembled. They are made of wood and can be erected in the most suitable place not only for the comfort and well-being of

the horse, but also to provide the easiest method of working from your point of view. Keep in mind the positioning of the muck heap, the distance from the hay and straw barns and the place where you would keep the fodder.

A loose box should be roomy enough for a horse to lie down easily without getting cast, and high enough to give plenty of head room. It should measure about 3·66m (12 ft) by 3·05 m (10 ft) for a pony, or 4·27 m (14 ft) by 3·66 m (12 ft) for a horse. Larger boxes may look nice, but they are more expensive to maintain and horses often seem to get into more trouble in a box that is too large than in one which is just about a comfortable size. The roof should slope away from the stable opening, and the stable doors must be high enough to prevent a horse from throwing his head up and banging his poll on the lintel. It is dangerous for horses to hit their heads, and particular care must be taken to ensure that the roof and door lintels are not too low.

The box should be light, airy and draught-proof because horses are very susceptible to draughts even though they can often withstand extremes of cold. Windows should be high up and preferably not in the side of the box opposite the door where they can create a cross-draught.

The siting of the box is also important. It should be placed on well-drained ground with its back to the prevailing winds, and have a solid floor made either of concrete or bricks. If it is made of concrete, the floor should be ridged slightly to prevent it from becoming slippery and, because drainage is needed, it should have a gentle slope towards the door with a gutter outside.

Doors must be in two parts and open outwards. The top half of the door can be opened to allow the horse to look out and also be fastened with a wall catch to prevent it from banging shut. Good ventilation is important. A grill across the top part of the doorway will allow plenty of fresh air at night without allowing a horse to get out. Ponies in particular can become very clever at getting over the bottom half of a door at night or when no-one is about.

The roof must be waterproof. Corrugated iron roofs are noisy in heavy rain and make a stable too warm in hot weather unless properly lined.

There should be as few interior fittings as possible, and there must not be any sharp edges. Mangers with edges are sometimes a problem because horses with a tendency to crib-bite and wind-suck can catch hold of them. For this reason it is wiser to use a strong round feed bowl which the horse cannot knock over and which can be removed for cleaning. There should also be on one of the walls a container to hold a lump of rock salt for the horse to lick.

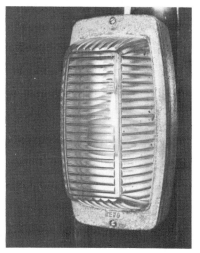

A strong ring is needed in the wall to which to tie the hay net high enough to prevent the hay seeds from getting into a horse's eyes and, in addition, room for two water buckets to be placed alongside one of the walls where they can be seen but not easily knocked over. Seeing the buckets every time you enter the stable or look over the door will probably remind you to keep them filled. All electric light fittings and switches should be of the safety variety.

A Tack Room for saddles and bridles, and a Fodder Store for feeding stuff, should be nearby, but hay and straw barns should be some distance away from the stables in case of fire.

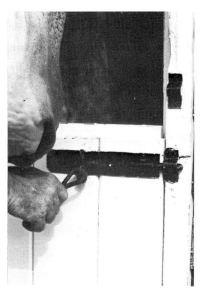

The essential needs of every stabled horse are a warm, dry stable, fresh air, exercise, good food of the right type, and plenty of clean water. The best bedding is wheat straw—which should be shaken out and spread knee deep to avoid the risk of capped elbows and hocks. This should be built up a little higher round the sides. It should be kept clean and dry and droppings removed regularly with a skip—hence the term 'skipping out'.

Unless you are using a deep litter the box should be cleaned out thoroughly *every* morning and, providing your horse is not due for early morning exercise, this can be done while he is tied-up enjoying his early morning hay net. You will find that he will then stand quietly while you get on with the job.

With a light fork, divide the clean straw from the soiled and pile it in a heap in the corner. The dirty straw and manure can then be taken away to the muck heap. In racing stables the lads often use sacks which have been cut along two sides and opened up to form a square. After the sacks have been filled with the dirty straw the stable lads pick them up with both hands by taking up each corner in turn, and swinging the sack over their shoulders. This is certainly a cheap and easy way of moving wet straw, but it can naturally be messy until you get the knack of picking the sacks up cleanly.

The stable floor should then be thoroughly swept with a hard broom, making sure that the drain is clear. If a box is not going to be used during the day, it can be washed down with a solution of water and disinfectant and then allowed to dry. But if it is required during the day, the clean straw should be spread out over the floor, and used as a base for fresh straw that will be needed when the horse is 'bedded down' in the evening.

Barley straw is used quite frequently nowadays. As the combine harvesters now remove most of the husks and soften up the stalks, there is little to choose between wheat and barley straw providing it is not damp or dusty.

Wood shavings and sawdust have also become popular forms of bedding—particularly if a horse is inclined to have respiratory troubles. This form of bedding is also cheap and easy to handle. Droppings must be removed quickly, however, before they can become trodden in, and the wet and dirty patches of bedding must be taken out every morning. A good covering of fresh sawdust or shavings needs to be put down every evening and spread evenly across the centre of the box with a wire rake. It is as well to bank some of the old bedding up round the sides of the walls, about 45·7 cm (18 ins) high, to give protection when the horse lies down.

Peat and bracken—and even shredded paper—are other forms of bedding which have been used successfully. Deep litter bedding is a labour-saving method whereby fresh straw is daily laid down over the old straw once the droppings have been picked up and the really wet or dirty straw has been removed. Sawdust is also sometimes used for 'deep litter'.

The box, however, must be large and airy. The accumulated litter needs to be cleared out at least every six to eight weeks— and the process started again. As the bed gets deeper the roof will become lower and so you must check that there is always enough headroom. Some owners are keen on the fact that the fermentation which sets up in the deeper layers of the straw generates heat and keeps the whole bed warm. However, there are mixed views on the benefits of 'deep litter'.

Above, left: saddles well arranged in the tack room. *Right:* a further view of the same tack room

The stable time-table must depend on the time you have available *each day*, and can be adapted to suit your individual needs as far as grooming and exercise are concerned. There must, however, be a regular routine. Horses are to a great extent creatures of habit, and they need feeding regularly and at the proper times. If you do not do this you have neither a happy nor a healthy horse.

The correct way to exercise has been dealt with in another chapter, but it is important to stress again that a healthy, active horse needs a steady two hours exercise a day – mainly walking and trotting, with short periods of cantering on suitable ground once he is really fit.

Regular grooming is, as already said, essential to the health and well-being of every stabled horse or pony because the skin is as vital to an animal's health as are his lungs and heart.

Grooming, known as 'quartering', should be done first thing in the morning. This is when the feet are picked out, the eyes, nostrils, and dock are sponged, and the rugs are unbuckled and turned back to allow a quick 'brush down' – done to make a horse look tidy before morning exercise.

After a horse has been exercised he will require a thorough grooming or 'strapping'. Because exercise warms up the skin, loosening and raising the scurf to the surface and opening up the pores, it is best to groom after a horse returns from work and is still warm.

Above: the clean straw is being forked into a corner

Above: making sure the stable floor is swept clean

Below: setting out for an exercise period.

Left: the manure is taken away in a barrow

4

Feeding and watering

Horses have small stomachs for their size and when they are allowed to roam freely they graze almost continuously so that their stomachs receive small quantities of food on a regular basis. They will also drink at frequent intervals relatively small amounts of water in between grazing.

A stabled horse, however, is normally fed several relatively large meals which will take longer to digest. If he drinks a lot of water soon after he has fed, because his stomach is so small, the food will be washed out into his intestine before it is really ready for the next stage of its digestive process. This can cause colic and other gastric troubles.

It is wise to make sure that a horse always has a plentiful supply of water in his stable. He can then drink whenever he wants to in the same way as he would if he was in his natural state. If a supply is not to hand, always water a horse before feeding – and do *not* water him again for at least two hours.

All horses need roughage, and the best basic food for a stabled horse is hay which also helps to provide the bulk needed to fill his rather large frame. The best is seed hay, harvested early in the summer before the seed and leaf has fallen. Hay made later may look equally good but it will lack the essential seed value and vitamins.

Good hay is greenish or light brown in colour, but not yellow. It should be crisp and sweet to the taste and have a fragrant aroma. Cheap, poor-quality hay which is dusty and has a musty smell will turn out to be the most expensive in the long run. Horses and ponies cannot cope with dust, and all sorts of digestive and respiratory troubles can result from bad hay.

Horses working hard will require a minimum of 4·5 kg (10 pounds or 5·4 kg (12 pounds) of hay a day, and this amount can increase to 6·8 kg (15 pounds) a day if the horse is in more strenuous work – such as hunting or eventing. Some owners allow their horses as much hay as they will eat and, providing the hay is of good quality and the animal does not become too fat, this is quite a sound practice.

Horses in gentle work – those perhaps only asked to exert themselves at weekends – can do quite well on hay supple-

Always make sure there is plenty of clean, fresh water in the stable

mented with small feeds of corn mixed with bran and chaff (which is hay and straw that has been finely chopped). Chaff is sometimes mixed with molasses to give it flavour.

If you want a horse to do any strenuous work, however, you will have to provide him with more protein. A horse which you are trying to get really hard and fit will need plenty of muscle-building food such as oats and barley. Some brands of good quality nuts are also rich in proteins, but it is as well to find out exactly what the nuts contain before feeding them.

Even if a horse is out at grass and you only want to use him at weekends, you will have to augment his grazing with hay and some protein feeds. It is much wiser to give him small feeds each day than to give him large feeds at the weekend – when he is expected to work. A good, daily supplementary ration for a 15·0 to 16·0 hand horse working weekends would be about 5·5 kgs (12 pounds) of hay with 1·4 kgs (3 pounds) of crushed oats or barley, 0·9 kgs (2 pounds) of bran, and one half a kilogram (1 pound) of chaff divided into two feeds and fed slightly damp. This diet needs to be varied according to the horse and the type of work you wanted him to do.

Always remember that ponies out at grass require plenty of good quality hay in the winter when there is little or no nutritious value in the grazing. They must also have a constant supply of fresh water all the year round.

Careful feeding is essential for stabled horses and ponies and a balanced diet must be worked out according to their temperaments and needs.

The best food for working horses is **oats** which should be short, plump and shiny with thin husks. They should always have a pleasant taste and smell, and weigh quite heavy in the hand. If you put some in your palm and grip the husks tightly they should spring apart, leaving a slight trace of flour when you open your hand. On no account feed oats which are dusty or which smell musty. Some people prefer feeding oats which have been crushed or bruised, but others like to feed the grains whole.

Bran is of little real food value, being the residue from milled wheat. It does, however, add bulk to a feed, and is good for the digestion because it makes the animal masticate his food. It should be dry, sweet and flaky. The broader variety is the best.

Barley is particularly useful as an alternative to oats, especially for ponies who may become rather too frisky when they are fed oats. It is also good for young animals, being an excellent bone builder. Because the husks are very hard, barley must always be crushed or boiled before being fed. The grains should be plump, short and hard. They must also be pale gold in colour and quite odourless.

Although oats, bran, barley and chaff can make up the main ingredients for a healthy diet, there are other alternatives which may be fed either to supplement the feed or perhaps make it more tempting.

Root crops, such as carrots, mangolds, swedes, turnips or even potatoes, are pleasant to feed, but they have little real food value. They must, however, always be sliced lengthways before being fed, otherwise they may become stuck in a horse's gullet. Raw potatoes make a good supplementary feed for horses or ponies who are gone in the wind.

Flake maize mixed with oats also makes a pleasant change of diet, though inclined to be fattening. **Sugar-beet pulp** has quite a lot of food value, but it must be soaked for at least 24 hours before being fed. **Linseed,** which is the seed of the flax plant, is an extremely useful addition to the fodder store, because it can be used in a variety of ways – including as linseed jelly, tea, gruel or mash. It must always be ground, boiled or soaked beforehand. Being rich in protein and fat, it should be used sparingly. It is useful as a tonic or when you want to improve the look of your horse's coat.

Food will keep better in vermin proof and damp proof bins

The concentrates provided in **horse and pony cubes** or **nuts** can save on time and labour because they provide a ready mixed diet. It is important to be absolutely sure that you know exactly what proteins you are feeding, however, and in what quantities. Some horses and ponies react differently to the various brands and mixtures of nuts, so feeding concentrates in this form is a matter of trial and error. Like the **vitamins** on sale for mixing with the feeds, they need to be used sensibly and not looked upon as being a lazy short cut to proper feeding.

All foodstuff should be kept in rat-proof and damp-proof bins. If you do get vermin in your fodder store, do not put down poison but use a trap, or better still, get a good stable cat. Poison can get on to the feet of vermin and become mixed with the feed. It is also important to remember that domestic pets, such as cats and dogs, can become poisoned themselves if they eat or even bite a rat or mouse that has eaten poison.

When you are planning a stable time-table, the basic rule must always be to feed little and often, and to restrict each feed to no more than 1·8 kgs (4 pounds), because the horse's stomach is not large enough properly to cope with bigger amounts. Try and vary the diet as much as possible. After all, no one likes eating the same thing meal after meal, day after day!

Successful dieting is a matter of finding out what is best for a horse or pony so that he remains fit and happy without becoming either too fat or too much of a handful.

To get an animal fit you should feed four meals a day with the main meal midday. If you can only feed three times a day, then cut out the afternoon feed. Horses must never be exercised until at least an hour after they have finished a meal. When you are competing, the feed times may have to be varied slightly accord-

Right: Making a bran mash. 1, add a little Salt to the bran; 2, put in boiling water with great care; 3, stir well; 4, place a sack over the bucket and allow the mash to cool before feeding

ing to the time of your particular class or event. If a horse does not seem to want all his feed, do not leave the food in the stable.

Try and give a horse a regular day off each week. On the evening before his rest day, when he should only have light walking exercise, give him a light laxative in the form of a bran mash. His regular feeds must be drastically reduced on his day off or he may become a victim of what is known as Azoturia, or 'Monday Morning Disease'. It was given that name years ago by the grooms looking after working horses which had been rested on Sundays without having had their regular feeds reduced sufficiently to take into account the fact that they would not be getting their usual exercise on that day. Azoturia is a very unpleasant illness which affects the muscles and can prove fatal.

Every owner should know how to make a mash. A **bran mash** is usually made in a bucket by pouring boiling water on to about 1·8 kgs (4 pounds) of bran which has been mixed with a touch of Salts, and stirred until it becomes a light paste. Put a sack over the bucket and leave the mash to cool for about 15 minutes.

A **linseed mash** is useful for putting some flesh on to a horse if he is in poor condition. Boil about a pound of linseed slowly for about three hours until all the grains become soft. The water left should be enough to soak up a pound of bran. Then add the bran paste to the cooked linseed and stir them both together into a thick paste which will then be ready to feed.

Linseed jelly is an excellent tonic which can be added to normal feeds. The linseed needs to be cooked very slowly for several hours. It will have to be stirred regularly to prevent it from becoming stuck to the side of the container until it turns into a jelly with a texture rather like that of starch. Drain away the water which can then be used as another good tonic – **linseed tea**. If you prefer to soak the linseed in water for about twenty-four hours it will also jellify. Decide which is the most convenient method. **Linseed gruel** is excellent for a tired horse. Cook the linseed in the way you would for a linseed mash, then strain it through a muslin to get rid of all the grain. You should feed it to a horse or pony immediately it is cool enough – before it turns to jelly.

If you do decide to change a horse or pony's diet you must do so gradually, otherwise he may develop colic – an illness of the digestive system sometimes referred to as 'gripes'. It can also be caused by poor quality food or too much cold water given when a horse is hot. The signs are: the animal will be in obvious pain, trying to kick at his belly, and looking round at his flanks. He will also want to lie down and roll. You should call the veterinary surgeon immediately and, while you are waiting for him to arrive, keep the animal warm and walk him around. The veterinary surgeon will probably recommend a draught made up of a stimulant mixed with something known as an opiate.

5

The care of a horse or pony at grass

Whether you are keeping a pony out at grass, or a Thoroughbred in a stable, there are basic rules to be observed to make sure he remains fit and happy, and that veterinary bills are kept to a minimum. Keeping a horse or pony is never cheap. The larger the animal the more he will cost to feed and stable. Add to that the cost of grazing, fencing, fodder, stable maintenance, tack and travelling, and the inevitable blacksmith's bills, you will appreciate why it is important to keep other costs – such as visits from your local veterinary surgeon – to within reasonable limits. Many mishaps and illnesses can be prevented by using a little commonsense and forethought.

Every horse or pony kept at grass all the year round should have at least 8 hectares (2 acres) of well-fenced and well-drained pastureland. The grass should be neither too lush, nor almost bare. Apart from an adequate supply of water, a pony will need a shed to protect him from the elements in winter and the flies in summer, and preferably some sort of stable where he can be taken if he becomes ill or suffers an injury.

Horses and ponies enjoy company and if you are planning to keep a pony on his own it is a good idea to find out whether anyone else in the area would be prepared to let your ponies graze together so that each will not only have some company, but also one field can be rested while the other is being grazed. Make sure that the other person's pony is fit and friendly before putting forward the suggestion – if all is well the idea can work quite successfully. If you find the right type of owner they will probably be willing to keep an eye on your pony for you if you have to be away, while you can do the same for them.

If you cannot do this – and you only have one large field for grazing – divide it in two so that one half can be rested while the other half is in use.

Never put a horse or pony into a field unless it is adequately fenced – either by stone walls, thick hedges, or with safe posts and rails about 1·2 m (4 ft) high. It is also important to ensure that a horse cannot get out on to a road where he can be involved in an accident, or perhaps get on to other land containing trees and plants which may be poisonous.

A shelter will be a protection in times of bad weather, and, in hot weather, a place in which a horse or pony can get away from flies

Ragwort is a common plant in meadows and hedgerows which can prove to be particularly poisonous even after it has been pulled from the ground. For this reason always make sure that you pull out cleanly any ragwort or other poisonous plants you may find in fields. Either burn them or throw the plants away somewhere where they cannot be eaten. Other dangerous plants, trees and shrubs include meadow saffron, horsetails, green bracken, St. John's wort, ground ivy, hemlock, water dropwort, foxgloves, yew, laburnum, rhododendrons, laurel, privet and acacia.

Although part of a large garden can sometimes be fenced-off to make a small paddock for use as an exercising area, ponies will need more space in which to graze. Never forget that when a field gets bare the pony will become bored and probably get into trouble.

Ponies never graze close to any of their own dung. You will discover that even though rich-looking clumps of grass grow up round the droppings, ponies will still not graze near them. If the field is small it is wise to pick up the droppings before they can get spread about and ruin a wider area for grazing. Sometimes spreading a layer of cow manure on to a field will counteract the effect of the horse droppings, and encourage the areas to be grazed.

Some plants and trees which are dangerous to horses and ponies when eaten in excess

Rhododendron

Yew

Hemlock

Privet

Ragwort

Foxglove

Horsetail

Buttercup

Oak

Ground Ivy

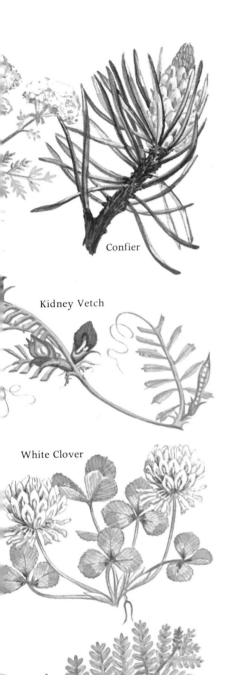

Confier

Kidney Vetch

White Clover

Bracken

The field will in any case need to be 'topped' frequently with a mowing machine to prevent coarse grass from forming, and to help promote a sweet, even growth of the shorter grass more attractive to a pony. A few heifers or bullocks will eat the coarser grass and also help to get rid of any red worm left by the horses, but if you do graze cattle always make sure you have really strong fencing because when one bullock or heifer manages to force a gap in a hedge and go through the others will follow.

Sometimes wire fences are inevitable, particularly if cattle are going to graze the fields when horses are not there. The wire, however, should be of plain heavy duty gauge and strained taut with the bottom strand at least a foot from the ground. Barbed wire fencing is not advisable because—apart from the problems of horses getting caught in any loose strands—the barbs can also play havoc with manes and tails.

Gates should be large enough to allow tractors to pass through easily or the field will be difficult to service. All gates should have good catches which are easy to open and close. Ditches in a field can be a problem. The shallow ones are safe enough, but the deeper ones, with straight sides, which a horse can fall or slide down into, should be fenced off.

A sound shed is necessary because trees which provide shelter in summer are bare of leaves in the winter and give little protection. The shed needs to be in good order, with plenty of head-room, and roomy enough for horses and ponies to move about freely. It should be placed in such a way as to provide protection from the prevailing winds, but make sure that if horses can get behind there is enough room for them to get out without getting cornered and being hurt. If there is a narrow gap behind the shed it is safest to fence off the potential trouble area with stout posts and rails.

The roof of the shed should preferably not be made of cor-rugated iron – which is inclined to get too hot in the summer and will discourage ponies from sheltering underneath at a time when they most need protection from the flies. Ensure that the entrance into the shed is wide enough for two full-size horses to pass through together without hurting themselves because, if they do get startled by anything while sheltering there, they may make a dash for the entrance and accidents can then occur.

In the spring the field will require a good harrowing – using a chain harrow to tear up the old grass and moss and let the air into the roots. A few days afterwards it should be rolled in order to even it out and get rid of any ridges and holes which may have been formed during the winter months.

A plentiful supply of clean water can best be provided by an automatic horse trough fitted with a ball-cock to regulate the flow, providing, of course, a piped water supply is laid on to the field. Old baths do not make good water containers because they are difficult to keep clean and horses are inclined to knock themselves on the rims. Whatever type of water container you use, it should not be placed under any trees where leaves can drop into the water which causes it to become sour.

Water will need to be checked every few days to see there is still a plentiful supply and nothing has happened to make it undrinkable. It is also a sound practice to walk round fields at regular intervals, not only to check the hedges or fencing but also to make sure that dangerous items like bottles, tins and old plastic containers have not been thrown into the field.

Unless a pony is one of the hardier Mountain and Moorland breeds, you will probably need a New Zealand rug if he is to be kept out in the winter in order to give him protection from the wind and rain. This is a weatherproof, canvas rug which has a surcingle and special leg straps to keep it in place when the animal gets down to roll. New Zealand rugs, however, need to be removed and readjusted morning and evening to prevent any discomfort and galling. It is also important that the rug should fit correctly and be of good quality so that it will not tear easily and lose its water-proofing qualities.

In summer months, some ponies – and particularly those of the Mountain and Moorland breeds – are susceptible to Sweet Itch – an irritable condition of the skin which occurs in the region of

Top: opening a gate
Above: ponies out at grass must have access to fresh water at all times

52

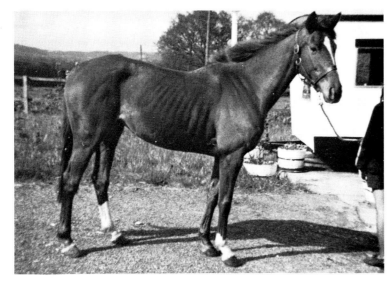

The importance of worming and proper feeding.
This Throughbred mare badly needed worming and had not been fed correctly.

Right: three weeks after being wormed and given correct diet and careful exercise she began to improve

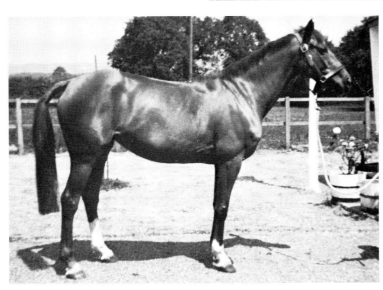

Left: after six weeks the mare showed her quality and was ready to go into training

the crest, withers and the croup. The pony can rub raw patches on his mane and tail in an effort to stop the irritation which is basically an allergic condition. It is also thought to be caused by insects of the biting variety. Lotions which can be rubbed into the areas likely to become affected every few days can be quite successful in preventing this miserable condition. There are also mixtures which will bring relief once a raw patch has been rubbed. If you see a pony rubbing his mane or tail, act quickly.

Warbles are also a nuisance, particularly in the spring when they develop as lumps beneath the skin on the back, usually in the saddle area. When this happens the maggot of the warble-fly will bore a small hole in the skin and then pop out. For this reason, warbles are best left alone until the maggot has made his departure, and then the small hole in the skin can be cleaned and healed by using wound powder or gall ointment. Afterwards the animal can be ridden by using a numnah with a hole cut to prevent the saddle from touching the affected area. If, however, the maggot is killed while still under the skin, a permanent and troublesome thickening can result. Never ride a horse or pony while a warble is developing.

In some countries bots can be another nuisance in the summer.

This rider has put a New Zealand rug on the pony before turning him out into the field

They appear as little yellow specks on a pony's legs, being caused when the gad fly or bot fly lays eggs on the legs when a pony is in the field. The pony then licks the eggs swallowing them and transferring them to the stomach where they hatch out. They are not really injurious, but if large quantities of eggs are swallowed in this way the pony can lose condition and develop a rather dry coat.

Most ponies will get bot eggs on their legs when they are out at grass during the summer months. If they are brought into the stable and starved for twenty-four hours, then given a drench made up of two tablespoonfuls of turpentine to a pint of pure linseed oil, the bots will usually be passed out of the body through the pony's droppings.

Whether a horse or pony is kept at grass or stabled, he will still need to be wormed frequently. Unless they are treated regularly, all ponies will suffer from worms. If this happens they will quickly lose condition, and much of the good food fed to them will be wasted on the worms. There are some sound worming products on the market which can either be mixed with the feed or taken through the mouth by way of a syringe. Your veterinary surgeon will be able to advise you if you are not sure of the best method to use.

Apart from regular visits from the blacksmith, horses and ponies also need their teeth examined at least every twelve months in order to make sure that they have not become too sharp and thus preventing the food from being digested properly. If the teeth are too sharp they will need rasping—and this is a job for an expert.

To get the best out of a horse or pony study him carefully and gain his confidence and respect. Every animal is an individual— and should be treated as such.

6

Bringing in a horse or pony from grass

Having purchased the horse or pony you feel will suit your needs and got him safely home, you may have had to turn him out into a field. When you go to catch him, however, you might then find that he has decided that he prefers the field – with the freedom it offers – and be determined to stay there.

If you are not sure that a pony will be easy to catch, always take a tit-bit with you, and if you think he may prove *really* difficult take a small bowl of pony nuts or oats.

Ponies which are difficult to catch should be turned out wearing a headcollar, unless they are going to be out at grass for some length of time. Always remember that the easiest time to catch a pony is when you first approach him. Once he has galloped round the field a few times, and made up his mind not be trapped, he will be much harder to catch.

Approach from the front or slightly to one side where the pony can see you, and walk towards his shoulder. Trying to creep up on him from behind will only startle him, and you will also be more likely to get kicked.

As you walk slowly, but firmly, towards him, don't forget to talk and encourage him. Give him confidence that there is nothing for him to be worried about.

If he is wearing a headcollar do not make a sudden grab for it when you think you are near enough, but stroke his neck until you can put your fingers through the noseband and slip the rope through the 'D' at the back of the headcollar.

Always use a rope to lead a pony. This is particularly important if you are leading him in traffic. If anything upsets or startles him and he twists away from your grasp, you will not have any chance of controlling him without a rope, and he may get loose in traffic with unfortunate consequences.

Hold the end of the rope with one hand, and take a firm hold of the other end – a short distance from the headcollar – with your other hand, palm downwards.

Unless you are walking along the left-hand side of the road lead from the 'nearside', that is the left-hand side of the pony if you imagine yourself standing at his tail and looking at his ears. His right-hand side would then be the 'off side'.

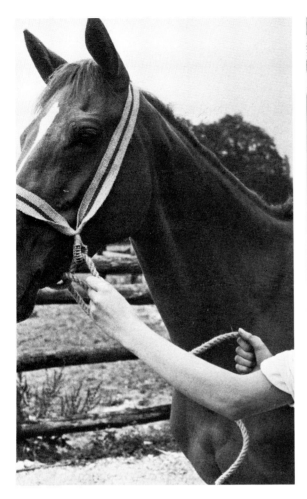

When using a halter a knot should be tied on the leading side where the rope runs through the loop in the noseband

To get the pony to move forwards speak to him quietly and walk forward yourself. Always look in the direction in which you want him to go, and not at the pony. Never try to 'pull him along'.

If you want to turn round, make sure that there is nothing coming behind you. Then check his pace, and move him round by pushing his head away from you. In this way the pony will remain balanced, with his head up, and you will be better able to control him.

If the pony does not have a headcollar you will need to use a halter with a rope already attached. After catching your pony, loosen the noseband of the halter and pass the rope gently over the pony's neck, speaking quietly to him as you do so. Then slip the noseband up over his muzzle, and the headpiece over his ears. Tie a knot on the leading side where the rope runs through the noseband. This will prevent the halter from becoming either too tight or too loose.

When you reach the stable, or the place where you are planning to groom and saddle up your pony, tie him up securely with a quick release knot of the type which will not become difficult

Right: the correct way to approach a pony and *(below)* to put on a head-collar

Right: after being caught the pony is led away

These pictures show a simple way
of tying a quick release knot
which will hold a pony quite
securely

The string loop will break without damage to the headcollar were the pony to pull sharply away

to undo if he pulls backwards for any reason. It is wise to loop a piece of string through the ring you are tying him to and then tie the rope to the string. If he does run back he will break the string and not the headcollar or halter.

Having caught and tied up your pony you will need to groom him before he is ready for your ride, but remember that when the time comes for you to turn him out again never let him gallop off the moment you get through the gate into the field. Turn him round to face the gate, give him a pat and then let him go free.

7

Grooming

Although grooming improves the appearance of a pony, there are more important reasons than this for a regular grooming routine. The skin is as vital to a pony's health as either his lungs or his heart, and grooming not only promotes health, it also helps maintain condition, prevents disease and ensures cleanliness.

When a pony is turned out during the winter months it grows a long coat which is very difficult to keep clean, and the grease and dandruff in the coat help to keep him warm and makes the hair more waterproof.

When the weather is cold and wet, grooming should be restricted to a good going-over with a dandy brush or a rubber curry comb to remove the worst of the mud. The pony's feet should, of course, be picked out regularly with a hoof pick, and the mane and tail kept tidy with a body brush. The pony's eyes, muzzle and dock will also need sponging with clean water, but that is really all that can or should be done in the winter months if the pony is out.

In the summer—or if the pony is stabled—he will need a thorough grooming to help keep him fit and well. Always groom to a system. In that way you will be less likely to forget anything.

Your grooming kit should be kept in a special box or basket. If you do not have one available, use a big canvas bag. Put all the items of grooming kit away carefully when you finish working. They will then be ready for you when you next need them, and all you will have to find is a bucket of clean water. Never leave brushes lying on the ground. They will only get dirty, and you will not get a clean pony with a dirty brush.

Begin by taking the hoof pick—that specially shaped piece of metal which will enable you to remove any stones or dirt which may have become lodged between the shoe and the frog. Picking up each foot in turn, work downwards with the hoof pick from the heel towards the toe. Clear the cleft of the frog—that 'V' shaped piece in the centre of the foot—and look for any signs of 'thrush' (an inflammatory condition noticeable mainly by a discharge and a foul smell). How to deal with ailments like thrush will be dealt with in another chapter.

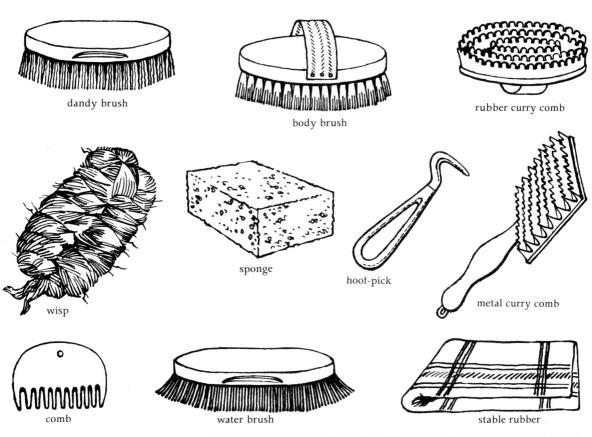

dandy brush

body brush

rubber curry comb

wisp

sponge

hoof-pick

metal curry comb

comb

water brush

stable rubber

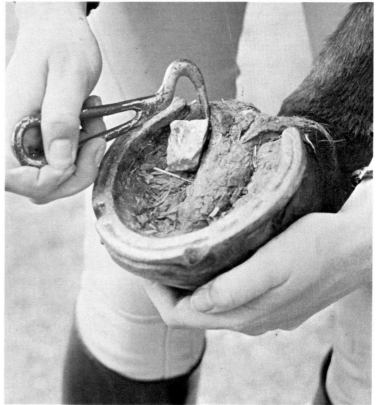

Stones can cause lameness and should be removed with a hoof pick

Getting to work with the dandy brush

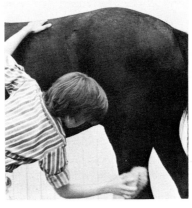

. . . not forgetting the legs

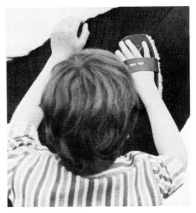

the body brush being used on the mane

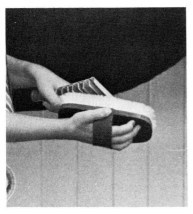

the brush needs to be scraped clean

. . . and the curry comb tapped clean on the floor

the headcollar must be looped round the neck

the wisp will help tone-up the pony

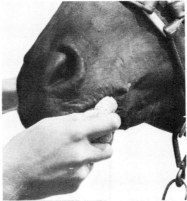

a damp sponge is used for the eyes, nose and mouth

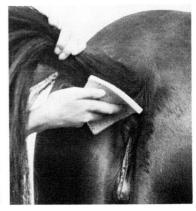

. . . and the dock area

. . . and getting dust out of the coat

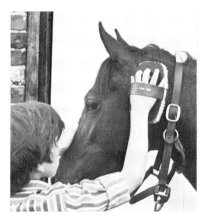

. . . before carefully brushing the pony's head

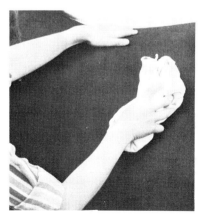

the stable rubber removes last traces of dust

Next, tap the shoe firmly with the handle of the hoof pick to make sure that it is secure. Finally run your fingers round the side of the hoof to see that all the nails are smooth, and none are sticking out to form what are called 'risen clenches'.

Because tidiness is important, it is a good idea to clean out the dirt and stones from the pony's hooves into what is called a dung skip–a round container or basket used for picking out droppings in the stable.

The really energetic part of the grooming now begins. Take the dandy brush–a wooden-backed brush with strong bristles– and remove all the caked dirt and sweat marks. Start at the top of the head and, using the brush in a to-and-from movement, pay particular attention to parts of the body such as the saddle region, the belly, and the points of the hocks and the fetlocks.

Change the brush over from one hand to the other and, if there is a lot of mud and the hair is long, you may find it easier to use a rubber curry comb in a circular motion.

When all the mud has been removed, exchange the dandy brush for the body brush. This is an oval-shaped brush of short, closely set bristles, with a thick band of webbing fixed to the sides to help you to hold it firmly.

Although the main purpose of the body brush is to remove dust and sweat from the body, neck and quarters, it is also used to keep the mane and tail tidy.

As you should always start at the front of a pony, begin with the mane by pushing it across to the wrong side of the neck and thoroughly brush the crest. Then, letting the mane fall back into its correct position, start at the withers, separating a few locks of hair at a time, and carefully brush out any tangles. Work slowly along the neck, only trying to deal with a few locks of hair at a time.

When you start removing the dust from a pony's coat the body brush will quickly become clogged unless you use a curry comb. This has a wooden handle and the comb is scraped across the body brush to remove the dust.

Take the body brush in the one hand and the curry comb in the other and, standing by the pony's neck on the near side, brush the coat in short circular strokes letting the brush go in the direction of the hair.

As you are doing this, stand well back from the pony and lean the weight of your body behind the brush, working with a slightly bent arm and supple wrist. After every few strokes remove the dirt from the body brush by drawing it smartly across the teeth of the curry comb, and then tapping the comb on the floor, behind the pony, and not on the stable wall.

After the near side has been finished, change over, and, using the curry comb and body brush, groom the pony's off-side.

When his body and legs have been brushed thoroughly, move

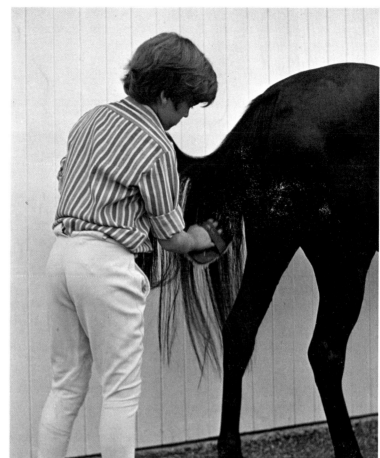

Left: a well-groomed pony,
saddled-up and ready for work
Above: using the body brush on
the tail

round to his head and slip off the headcollar. You can still keep
him tied safely by buckling the headstrap loosely round his neck.

Ponies are usually quite happy to have their heads groomed
gently, but they will resist any rough treatment. The curry
comb will not be needed when you are brushing a pony's head.
Thus with one hand you can hold him still and, holding the brush
in the other, work away quietly, trying to avoid any tender
areas or bony projections. When you have finished, the headcollar can be replaced, and the body brush given a final clean
on the curry comb.

The only part left to do now will be the tail. In the same way
as you did the mane, tackle only a few locks of hair at a time and

brush out the tangles. The easiest way is to hold the tail in one hand and shake out a few hairs at a time with your fingers. Use the body brush on the tail and never the dandy brush which will only tend to remove or break the hairs.

It is not time, however, for you to stand back and admire the results, because your pony still needs a massage to help harden up his muscles. A massage will also improve his blood supply and produce a shine on his coat by squeezing oil from the glands of his skin. This body massage can either be done with a wisp, a tightly-woven rope of twisted-up hay or straw, or with a special leather pad.

The wisp should be dampened slightly with water and used vigorously by bringing it down with a bang in the direction of the lay of the coat. Pay special attention to those parts where the muscles are hard and flat—such as the sides of the neck, the quarters and thighs—but take care to avoid the tender region of the loins and any bony prominences. As you bring the wisp down in a steady, rhythmic movement you should be able to see the muscles twitch. Most of the really hard work is now over, but you have not finished yet.

Wring out the sponge in a bucket of clean water to make sure that it is soft, clean and damp. Then, holding your pony's head still, gently sponge his eyes—moving away from the corners and around the eyelids. Clean the sponge and wipe the muzzle region —including the lips and the inside and outside of the nostrils.

Wring out the sponge once more and, lifting the pony's tail as high as you can, clean the whole of the dock area, including the skin underneath the tail. This is most important because sponging helps to refresh a pony. He will probably appreciate this more than any other part of the grooming routine.

While you have the water bucket handy 'lay' the mane by dipping the end hairs of the water brush in the bucket and, after shaking away the excess water, lay the hair flat by brushing it from the roots downwards.

Unless the weather is extremely cold and frosty, the water brush can also be used to wash a pony's feet. If you do wash his hooves, it is important to keep the thumb of the hand holding the pony's foot pressed well into the hollow of the heel to prevent water from becoming lodged there.

When the hooves are dry they will be ready to be oiled. A small brush dipped in a jar of hoof oil is the best way of doing this. Oil will not only improve the appearance but also help prevent brittle or broken feet.

Finally, take a slightly dampened stable rubber and go all over the pony's coat to remove the last traces of dust.

Allow plenty of time for grooming. An experienced groom will usually take about forty minutes, but remember that if it is going to be effective it must be done thoroughly each day.

8
Saddlery and equipment

When anyone mentions saddlery you will probably immediately visualise the saddles and bridles, girths, stirrups and leathers in use every day. People rarely stop to think of the wide variety of the bits, martingales and other equipment which are available to riders to help make their horses and ponies more comfortable to ride and, in addition, easier to control.

A well-fitting saddle and bridle is essential if you expect a horse or pony to be comfortable and at the same time be in the right frame of mind to carry out your wishes without resistance. No horse can be expected to give of his best while being subjected to saddlery which is either ill-fitting or unsuitable for his particular action or temperament. The first thing you must do is to check your saddlery and make sure it fits and is of the correct type.

Saddles

Start with the saddle. A badly fitting saddle will cause discomfort to both you and the horse and can seriously hamper his movements. Horses, like humans, may look similar in build, but they are never completely identical in shape or character, and for this reason it is best for every horse to have his own saddle which can be allowed to settle down and mould to the shape of his back.

The term 'All Purpose' or 'General Purpose' which is given to a saddle means that it is suitable for a variety of uses—such as hacking, hunting or jumping. It does not mean that it will fit every type of horse. Quite the opposite is often the case and, if you do use the same saddle on different horses, it will eventually not fit any of them correctly, and the horses will almost certainly end up with sore backs.

A first-class horse or pony deserves a good saddle. There is after all little sense in spending time, money and effort in schooling him properly, and getting him fit and well, if you are going to spoil everything by not providing him with a saddle which will be comfortable for you both.

Quite apart from your own comfort—and making sure that the saddle in no way retards your horse's freedom of movement—remember that pressure and friction are the two most frequent

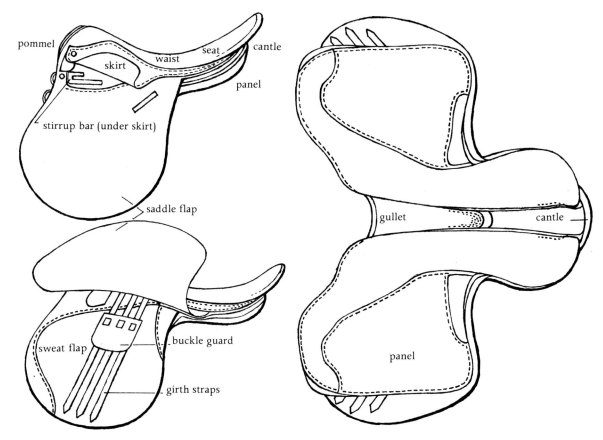

causes of soreness and must be avoided at all costs. The first
essential is to see that the tree of the saddle fits correctly. Take a
look at the diagram of the saddle and you will see the names
given to the various parts. The tree on which the saddle is made,
is usually in three sizes—narrow, medium and broad.

Although a good saddler can sometimes make a narrow tree
broader, he cannot successfully make a broad tree narrower. At
least his efforts will not prove to be successful in the long run,
and so it is not really worth trying. Attempting to put more
stuffing into the front of a saddle with too broad a tree will only
tend to throw the saddle out of balance, and taking stuffing out
of a narrow saddle to try to make it fit a broader animal will be
equally ineffective. If the saddle is too narrow the points of the
tree will pinch and cause soreness, and if it is too wide, the arch
will bear down on the withers and again cause discomfort.
Modern trees allow for quite a lot of flexibility in fitting, and if
the saddle also happens to have a sloped back head, it can
probably be made to fit quite a number of horses. However, once
the right fit has been achieved it is best to stick to the rule of
one saddle, one horse.

It is wise to get the advice of a competent saddler if you are not
sure whether a saddle really fits because getting it right can save
a lot of problems later on. When you have checked that the tree

Above: a saddle resting on a saddle horse

is the correct size, the next task is to see that the saddle gives complete clearance of the withers and along the backbone. Sit in the saddle and check whether you can put three fingers between the forearch of the saddle and the horse's withers. If you cannot, there will not be enough clearance for comfort.

While you are still in the saddle get someone to check that the underneath panel bears evenly across either side of the animal's back, also that the channel of the panel is deep enough and wide enough to be clear of the backbone at all paces and when you are jumping. It is important, however, while noting that there is not undue pressure in the wrong places, to check that the saddle still fits snugly and is as close to the horse's back as possible.

Saddles need re-stuffing at regular intervals because the weight of the rider will in time make the panel flat, so that there is not enough clearance in the channel. To prevent this from happening, take the saddle to a really good saddler. He will be able to re-shape it for you.

Badly fitting saddles are, of course, not the only cause of sore backs. Stable rollers with pads so flat that they are bound to put constant pressure on a horse's spine, and are then done up too tightly, can cause a considerable amount of trouble. Putting some sacking or a rubber pad under the roller is not the real answer. It is essential that a horse's backbone should be free of pressure at all times, and so the roller should be stuffed and fitted in the same way as you would for a saddle.

Saddles which are too long in the tree put too much pressure on the loins and, apart from soreness, may also cause irreparable damage to the horse's kidneys. If a large rider sits in a saddle which is too small, his weight will be concentrated over too restricted an area of the horse's back and cause similar problems.

In the case of a fat pony kept out at grass—where it is more difficult to keep him to a diet—you may be faced with the problem of a saddle which continually rides forwards over the withers, making it not only uncomfortable for the pony, but also very disconcerting for the rider. The only real solution is a crupper which will go under the pony's tail and fasten on to the back of the saddle.

The crupper can be adjusted according to the saddle and the size of the pony. A serge-lined saddle, instead of a leather-lined one can also sometimes be of help. Numnahs and wither pads should never be regarded as a permanent solution to an ill-fitting saddle.

Some riders like using a numnah because they feel it acts as an additional cushion between the saddle and the horse's back. Others, however, are of the opinion that a numnah quickly becomes saturated with sweat, and can cause overheating, leading to a sore back. Providing a saddle fits well and the panels are maintained properly, there seems little reason for a numnah which will, if anything, place a rider further away from his horse and not give him the correct feel. If you do use a numnah, however, the best is probably the type made of plastic foam which does not cause heating of the back, and is relatively easy to keep clean.

Wither pads are more usual in racing circles, although they can be used as a temporary measure if a saddle has begun to sink in the front and until it can be restuffed properly.

If you need a new saddle and it is difficult for your saddler to come and see your horse or pony, there is a useful way of measuring a horse's back. You will need a thick piece of lead – or a thick piece of wire – about 46 cm (18 ins) long. This should be shaped over the withers of the horse at about the place where you would expect the front or head of the saddle to be. Press the wire down until it forms the shape of the back, and then transfer it to a piece of paper so that the outline can be traced. Repeat – only this time take the measurement back about 4 cm (10 ins) from the first measurement – and then to complete the job take the final measurement along the length of the back from the withers. If you add to this details of your own height, weight, and inside leg measurement to the knee, your local saddler will have quite a lot of information to go on in suggesting a suitable saddle.

There are a number of different types for you to choose from, depending on what you want to do. A General Purpose saddle will have a wide variety of uses, or you may require a Show Saddle, a Hunting Saddle, a Dressage Saddle (with its straight front), or a Jumping Saddle (with its forward cut). A Child's Saddle can vary from a felt pad to a smaller version of the General Purpose saddle. Some have a full panel and others a short panel – which is meant to allow the small rider to have a better 'feel' and grip.

Every saddle needs a good sound girth to hold it in place. These usually vary – from about 92 cm (36 ins) for a small pony to 1·35 m (54 ins) for a large horse. They are made of leather, web, lampwick, or nylon cord. The most expensive, but undoubtedly the best, are those made of leather, providing that they are properly looked after and kept nice and supple.

Leathers
Stirrup leathers are made of either cowhide, rawhide or buffalo hide. All leathers stretch, and rawhide and buffalo hide will frequently stretch more than cowhide. As riders usually place more weight in one stirrup iron than the other, especially when mounting, the leathers ought to be changed over at regular intervals to ensure that one does not become more stretched than the other. Because all new leathers will stretch, they should never be worn for competitions or hunting until they have had time to settle down.

1

2

Bridles and bits
1, a Kimblewick shown with a 'Flash' noseband and standing Martingale. The throat lash here needs tightening a hole or two; 2, a Pelham, used with a Cavesson noseband. The throat lash here appears to need loosening a hole or two; 3, a bitless Hackamore; 4, a Double bridle

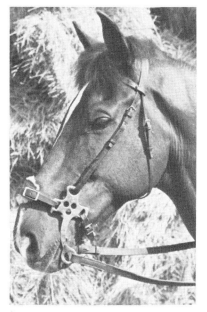

3

4

Stirrup irons

Stirrup irons should preferably be made from stainless steel, and they must always be large enough to let boots go in and out without hinderance. A good, heavy stirrup iron will also free the foot more easily in the event of a fall.

Bridles

There are five main types of bridle. Apart from the snaffle—which is the most common of all—there is the Pelham, the Weymouth, the Gag and the Bitless Bridle. Although bridles may have different bits, they all have a headpiece which includes the throatlash to prevent the bridle from slipping over the horse's head; cheek pieces which buckle on to either side of the headpiece (and to which the bit is secured), the browband which helps to hold the headpiece in place; the Cavesson or noseband to which a standing martingale can be attached, and the reins.

In a Double bridle the bridoon or snaffle bit is secured by a secondary strap and cheekpiece, which passes through the slots of the browband. The Double bridle and the Pelham both have two pairs of reins and a lipstrap which passes through a ring on the curb chain and keeps it in place in the curb groove.

Nose bands

A plain Cavesson is always used with a Double bridle, but there are various other nosebands, such as the elegantly stitched ones used mostly for showing, the sheepskin-covered nose bands—originally used in the United States of America to prevent trotting horses from shying, but which are now popular among racehorse trainers and show jumpers—and the Drop nose band which is fastened round the muzzle below a snaffle bit in order to prevent a horse from pulling and also to ensure that he cannot open his mouth far enough to hang out his tongue.

There is also a 'Flash' nose band—an ordinary Cavesson nose band with two diagonal crossing straps sewn on to the centre which also are fastened beneath the bit. It is used instead of an ordinary Drop nose band when a standing martingale is required.

Reins

The reins can be made of leather, web, plaited nylon or plaited cotton, although leather reins are sometimes covered in rubber to give a better grip when hunting or show jumping. The rubber covering should be stitched by hand with a large spot stitch down the centre. In time, the rubber will rub smooth and need to be replaced by the saddler. Web reins also provide a good grip in wet weather, but whereas the soft plaited cotton reins are excellent in most conditions the plaited nylon reins are inclined to stretch and slip.

The normal length of a full size rein is about 1·5 m (five feet), but reins used on children's ponies are usually much shorter or they would be inclined to hang down in a loop which could catch the rider's feet.

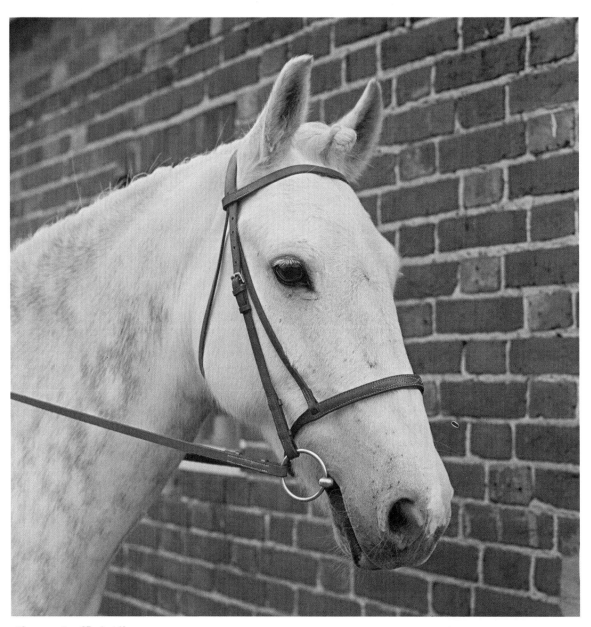

Above: a Snaffle bridle

Right: the girth is put through the
loop of the Martingale to hold it
in place

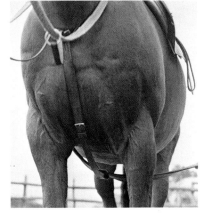

Martingales

Martingales are sometimes needed to help lower a horse's head.
They give the rider more control by preventing any evasion of
the bit, and are frequently used in jumping—if a horse's head
can be held low and the neck can still be stretched he will jump
with a round, supple back and be less likely to hit a fence than he

would if he flung up his head and hollowed his back. If the martingale is too tight, however, the horse will not have enough freedom to extend his neck outwards and downwards when he is jumping. His ability to jump spread fences will then be seriously impaired.

There are four main types of martingale. The standing martingale which has a loop at either end – one of which fastens on to the girth through the forelegs and the other on to the noseband. Like all but one of the martingales, it has a neck strap to keep it in position. Then there is a running martingale which again fastens on to the girth, but the other end has rings for the reins to pass through. If a running martingale is used with a double bridle, the bridoon or snaffle rein is passed through the rings.

The bib martingale is rather like the running martingale, but has a triangular piece of leather sewn between the branches holding the rings to prevent an excited horse from getting himself caught up in the branches. The Irish rings look rather like a pair of spectacles, and are sometimes called Irish martingales. They do not affect the position of the horse's head, but they prevent the reins from going over his head – particularly during a fall.

Another martingale which is still popular in some areas is known as the Market Harborough. This is brought into action not by the rider, but by the movement of the horse's head. When a horse carries his head correctly the Market Harborough becomes inoperative, but when he starts to throw it up there is a downward pull on the bit and on the bars of the mouth. It is really a sophisticated form of draw rein which was fastened to the girth on either side, through the rings of the bit and back to the rider. Under show jumping rules a Market Harborough may only be used with a snaffle.

Bits

Bits help to impose control on a horse by putting pressure on the corners and bars of the mouth, the tongue, the poll, the nose, the roof of the mouth and the curb groove. The object of a bit is to assist the rider to position his horse's head to give maximum control over speed and direction. Various bits act in various ways, and there is a wide variety from which to choose – ranging from the plain jointed snaffle to the Double bridle, with its two bits and double reins.

Double bridle

The Double bridle should never be used by an inexpert rider. In the wrong hands it can cause a horse both discomfort and possible harm. It consists of the bridoon or snaffle, below which is fitted the curb bit with its curb chain and lip strap. The bridoon is usually jointed and the curb has a straight bar mouthpiece with an upward bend in the middle, known as the port. The correct positioning of the horse's head is achieved by raising the head with the snaffle, and lowering it and bringing the nose inwards by means of the curb. In Britain the bridoon rein is usually held on the outside of the rider's little finger – and outside the curb rein to emphasise the action of the bridoon – but in France the bridoon rein is held between the third and fourth finger, and the curb rein under the little finger – which puts more emphasis on the curb bit. In this way, the reins correspond to the position of the bridoon and the curb bit in the animal's mouth.

The Pelham is a cross between a snaffle and a double bridle. It uses two reins, but the mouthpiece is a mullen one of either metal or vulcanite and fitted with a curb chain. Children sometimes use a Pelham with leather roundings which join the snaffle and curb rings so that a single rein can be used.

In many countries the Kimblewick is an even more popular bit for children because it is really a form of Pelham with a straight bit, having a small port, short cheek-pieces, and a curb chain, but using a single rein.

An Irish martingale, or 'Irish rings'

The Gag is really an exaggerated snaffle, but the rings have holes in the top and bottom through which goes a cheekpiece of rounded leather with the reins attached. It is particularly helpful on horses who approach their fences too quickly, with their heads held low.

If you want to check the size of a bit, remember that snaffle bits are measured between the rings when laid flat. A mullen mouthpiece is also measured between the rings.

Most varieties of Bitless bridle combine pressure on the nose with pressure on the curb groove, and they have cheekpieces which are sufficiently long to give the rider considerable leverage. They are extremely useful for a horse or pony whose mouth may have been so ruined that he will not go well in any other type of bridle.

Saddlery must always be well-looked after. It is expensive and should be made to last. It must also be kept in good order from the point of view of safety. Broken stitching or brittle leather straps can prove a menace. It is up to the rider to make sure that his or her equipment is both checked and cleaned properly and regularly. Cleaning tack need not be a chore. If the weather is fine it can be done outside – the task will then seem much more enjoyable.

Water, heat and neglect are the three things which will ruin leather quicker than anything else. Leather loses a percentage of its fat content every day – and the heat and sweat from a horse's body will quickly help to make leather dry and brittle and ready to crack.

Saddles and bridles and other items of leather equipment should be cleaned with a damp sponge after every use and then

A Grakle noseband needs to be carefully fitted

finished off with saddle soap which should be applied with a slightly damp sponge. Do not put too much grease on the outside of your saddle, because it will not be absorbed and will only dirty your breeches. About once a week go over all the leather with one of the preparations on the market for keeping leather supple, but be careful not to overfeed the leather otherwise you will make it flabby and greasy. Always take a bridle to pieces to clean it, and undo all the buckles on the stirrup leathers and martingales.

Bits, stirrup irons and curb chains will need washing in warm soapy water, and then be given a good polish with a dry cloth.

Apart from the saddlery needed for riding your horse, you will also have to think about equipment for the stable. A good stable headcollar is the first essential. Try not to buy a cheap one with galvanised or tinned buckles, because a brass mounted headcollar, with a rolled leather throat strap – and at least two rows of stitching on the cheeks and back stay – will always look smarter and, in addition, last longer. If you have a small pony a Dutch Slip or even a yearling headcollar, which is adjustable, will sometimes do quite well. Whatever type of leather headcollar you use, however, do not forget that it will need cleaning.

It is also useful to have a pad for protecting your horse's poll when he is travelling. This is a felt pad with slots through which the head strap of the headcollar can be passed to hold it in place, but the headcollar must have a browband to prevent the pad from sliding over the horse's head.

You will also need a stout rope fitted with a safety hook to clip on to the metal square at the rear of the headcollar when the horse is tied up or being led, although some prefer to use rack chains in the stable. If your horse is inclined to run backwards when he is tied up, you will have problems with broken headcollars. The immediate answer – until you can cure him of the habit – will be a strong rope halter, preferably of the type which has a throatlatch to stop it from getting pulled over the eyes.

Water buckets, hay nets and a feed bowl of the larger metal variety which cannot be knocked over are also needed in a stable. Large plastic or rubber buckets which are easy to keep clean are quite adequate. They do not become slimy like the wooden buckets, and are less heavy, and they do not rattle like metal ones if they get kicked or knocked over. Hay nets are invaluable because – apart from enabling hay to be weighed before being fed – they also prevent waste, as the animal can pick out a mouthful at a time. This discourages him from eating too quickly with the result that the hay does not get trodden into the bedding or kicked around the box – as it would do if it was fed on the floor.

You must make sure you hang the net up high enough to prevent the seeds from getting into a horse or pony's eyes and keep it out of the way of his legs when it becomes empty. To ensure this, pull the neck cord tight when the net has been filled and put the loop through the hay net ring on the stable wall until it is the correct height. Then thread the end of the loop through two or three of the strands of cord near the bottom of the haynet and pull it upwards until you can tie it through the ring with a quick release knot. In this way the haynet will be tied up double and will not hang low when empty.

Hay nets made of tarred cord are meant to prevent a horse from chewing the netting. This is usually rather a forlorn hope, but if you have to dampen down your horse's hay the tar does help prevent the cord from rotting too quickly. Of course, all nets will rot in time if they are constantly subjected to water.

When you are feeding hay in a field use a hay rack to prevent waste.

Another important stable item is a skip for removing droppings. The basket types are light and easy to use, and a deep one is particularly handy. There are also some plastic and rubber muck skips which are quite satisfactory.

This young rider is being shown the correct way to tie up a hay net

When you start buying rugs you will have to decide exactly what you want because, apart from being expensive, they take up a considerable amount of room and need regular attention if they are not to become both worn and torn.

The most important rug—if a horse is stabled—is without doubt a night or stable rug, usually made from jute and lined with blanketing. There are, however, some other types of proprietary night rugs on the market which will also do the job quite adequately. Always try to buy rugs which are of really good quality. They will without doubt last longer and stand up to washing. Night rugs are certain to get dirty and become stained with dung and a cheap rug that tears and rots easily—and cannot stand up to being washed properly—will not last, and will turn out to be more expensive in the long run.

Some rugs have their own surcingles in addition to a breast strap, but others will require a well padded roller to keep them in place. Some of the better night rugs have eyelets at the rear to allow for a tail string to prevent the rug from sliding forward. Rollers should always be fitted very carefully. They are usually about four to five inches wide, and can be made of hemp web, jute web, wool web, or leather.

If a horse is stabled he will also need a good blanket to go under the night rug in winter. These can be expensive and these rugs are usually priced according to their weight.

An anti-sweat rug is not only useful in the stable when a horse has returned from exercise and is still sweating up, but is a very handy rug to have to hand when travelling. It is made of large cotton mesh—and works on the same principle as a string vest by creating air pockets next to the horse's body and be-

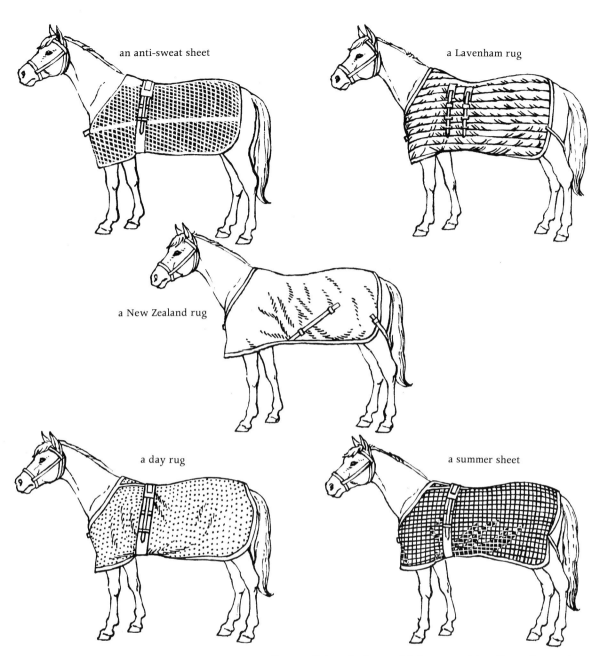

an anti-sweat sheet

a Lavenham rug

a New Zealand rug

a day rug

a summer sheet

Rugs

comes a form of insulation which stops him from becoming chilled. These rugs should always be used with an additional top sheet, otherwise the insulating air pockets cannot be formed, and the rug is of little use—except perhaps to keep off the flies! It should be kept in place with a roller because it will tear easily if the horse rolls—and the rug becomes displaced.

The wool day rug is like the night rug in shape, but it is available in different colours and bindings. You can have your initials sewn on either side of the rug—at the bottom end corner. The rugs look smart, particularly for travelling.

Summer sheets help to keep away dust and flies. They are made of cotton or linen and, like all the other rugs, need to be kept in place with a surcingle or roller. Horses travelling can also do with the extra protection of a tail guard–made of soft leather or canvas. It goes over the tail bandage and is fastened on to the roller.

New Zealand rugs have become almost a necessity because they not only provide protection for a horse or pony which has been trace-clipped and is at grass, but they also give sufficient warmth and covering for a hunter to be turned out into a field when the weather is reasonably good and it is not possible for him to be exercised. New Zealand rugs must be fitted carefully because–being made of strong waterproof canvas and lined with blanketing–they can slip and cause chaffing around the neck area when a horse rolls. Care should be taken when removing the rugs to undo the leg straps first, and buckle them out of harm's way. New Zealand rugs require regular attention because they lead a hard life, having to withstand all winds and weathers, and probably being brushed against branches and hedgerows. The leather straps need regular greasing or they will become too hard, and the fastening hooks will also require oiling to avoid corrosion.

Putting on a working bandage

In Britain day rugs and stable rugs are measured from the centre of the breast to the back of the rug, and usually range in size from about 1·2 m (48 ins) to 1·8 m (72 ins).

The types of bandages and boots required depend not only on the type of work you want a horse to do–and whether this will involve travelling–but also on his behaviour when jumping or in fast work. The main function of boots and bandages is both to protect the legs against injury and to provide some support to the tendons. Brushing, when the inside of the leg, usually in the region of the fetlock joint, knocks against the opposite foot, and over-reaching, when the hind toes strike into the back part of the foreleg, can often be caused by poor shoeing producing a faulty action. This is not always the case, however, and the use of boots or bandages to prevent these types of injuries from occurring will then become a necessity.

Jumpers also sometimes need protection against the knocks they receive when hitting an obstacle, particularly when schooling, and this can take the form of either bandages, boots and jumping kneecaps, or sometimes all three. There are also special boots to protect all four legs of polo ponies from being struck by either a stick or the ball.

The lighter type of five strap leather or felt brushing boot will provide adequate protection against occasional brushing, although one of the simplest and yet most effective anti-brushing devices is the rubber ring. When a horse is in fast work the point of his fetlock at the rear can come into contact with the ground and, if that happens, a heel boot will be needed. Over-reaches when jumping mostly occur low down on the heel. The best

80

The tail bandage covers the top part of the tail

protection against this is the rubber over-reach boot which should be made of almost pure rubber so that it is elastic enough to pull over the hoof but small enough to fit snugly on the foot without revolving. A more dangerous form of injury can occur about the joint and in the back of the tendon. To prevent this a tendon boot should be worn. This has a strong pad at the rear, shaped to the leg, which will also help to support the tendon. Shin boots are also used on jumpers to protect their front and hind legs.

When travelling, felt hock boots safeguard a horse against banging his hocks on the side of the box, and travelling knee-caps, which are sometimes also used at exercise, will give protection to a horse's knees. They should, however, be loose enough to give freedom of movement.

Bandages come into two categories. Those of the stretch variety, which give support under working conditions, and those that provide warmth and protection when travelling. Exercise and working bandages, which give a degree of stretch, must always be put on over gamgee tissue, and should be sewn in place when being used for cross-country riding or eventing.

Some riders now prefer a type of elasticated sock—rather like the surgical stocking sometimes worn by men and women. They are made in various shapes and sizes, and can be used for veterinary purposes to hold leg dressings in place.

Working bandages, used on the front legs, are put on between the knee and the fetlock joint, and on the hindlegs between the fetlock and the hock, whereas stable and travelling bandages, which are made of wool, envelope the whole joint, and are sometimes put on over protective foam rubber pads.

Finally let us take a look at three of the artificial aids we have not yet mentioned—namely whips, canes and spurs. There are a wide variety of whips produced for various uses and at various prices, ranging from the cheaper type of general purpose whip with a fibreglass centre, to the hunting whips with their plaited leather thongs and cord lashes.

Sticks or canes covered with leather are popular for showing, and are perhaps better than a whip for the novice rider because they can also help maintain the correct hand position. The maximum length of stick allowed when show jumping is 30 centimetres.

Spurs are always worn with hunting boots, but if spurs are worn for schooling or jumping they should always be of the blunt type (with a curved neck which can vary in length up to about one and a half inches). Some experienced riders wear spurs for schooling which have finely-pointed rowels. Used by someone who knows exactly what he is doing, they can mean less discomfort to a horse than the bruising produced by a blunt-type being continually thumped into a horse's sides by a novice.

9
Saddling and unsaddling

After you have caught and groomed your pony he will be ready for his saddle and bridle. Make sure, however, that your smartly groomed pony is securely tied-up before you leave him to go and fetch his tack. If you do not you may return to find that he has either wandered off, or has got down and had a good roll!

Check that saddle and bridle are ready for use before leaving the tack room. It is far easier to check a saddle on a saddle rack than when it is on the back of a fidgety pony.

Make sure that the stirrup irons and leathers are secure on the saddle—with the irons run up—and that the girth is already attached to the girth tabs on the off-side of the saddle.

The bridle should already have been adjusted so that it will be large enough to fit over the pony's head. If it is too small, alter the straps or find a larger bridle.

Good saddles and bridles are expensive and they need to be carried properly to prevent them from being damaged by being dragged along the floor or scraped against a wall. The easiest way is to hold the saddle with the front arch in the crook of your elbow so that you can carry the bridle over the same shoulder leaving your other hand free to open doors or deal with the pony. Some people prefer to carry the saddle along their thigh—with their hand in the front arch to hold it in place. It is mainly a matter of deciding which way is the most comfortable.

Approach the pony from the near-side, and speak to him so that he knows you are there.

If the pony wears a martingale, put this on first, but if he only has a saddle and bridle it is correct to put the saddle on before the bridle. There is a very good reason for this. The saddle—providing it fits correctly—will settle into a pony's back, and the heat from his body will help to warm the underneath part before you mount.

Many horses and ponies 'blow themselves out' when the saddle is being put on. This is because they think the saddle will be done up too tightly, and they take a deep breath to guard against this.

Never do the girth up tight immediately. How would you like a cold saddle put on your back and tightened up all in one go?

Carrying a saddle and bridle in the correct manner

You would hate it . . . and so will a pony. When you place the saddle on his back, take it in the crook of your left arm, and put it well forward of his withers, then slide it back into position, making sure with your right hand that the hair underneath the saddle is lying smoothly.

Your girth should be lying across the saddle already fastened on the off-side. Then, when you let the girth drop, you can lean underneath the pony's belly and bring the loose end up to be fastened.

Always keep near a pony's shoulder so that you will be out of harm's way if he does kick out for any reason. You will also be less likely to be in a position to get a nip.

Check that the sweat flap is down and, before doing up the girth, let it drop loose and walk round the front of the pony to the off-side to make sure that nothing is ruffled up under the saddle flap. Then go back to the near-side and keeping your own shoulder close to the pony's shoulder, tighten the girth just enough to hold the saddle firm, making sure that you have not pinched any of his skin. When you are ready to mount up and you tighten the girths, there should be approximately the same number of holes on either side.

Next take hold of the bridle which should have been hung up out of harm's way. If you have to saddle-up in a field, without anywhere to hang the bridle, you can always keep it out of the way by putting it over your left shoulder. Place the bridle with your left hand under the brow-band and headpiece, so that the brow-band is nearest to your elbow. Then put the buckles of the reins in front of the headpiece onto your left forearm, leaving both hands free to undo your pony's head rope.

As soon as you do this he will usually try and put down his head and look around for something to eat, but you must be ready for him. You cannot put a bridle on a pony when his head is on the floor.

After undoing his rope, put the reins over the pony's neck with your right hand so that you will have something to hold him with if he tries to walk away when you undo his headcollar or halter. If possible, place the halter on a convenient peg or hook, and try not to put it on the ground where it can be trodden on by you or the pony. There is no point in getting it damaged or dirty.

If you are in a stable or stall, turn the pony round into the light. Hold the headpiece of the bridle with your right hand, leaving yourself free to slide your left hand under the pony's mouth with the bit resting across your fingers and thumb.

The pony may not want to open his mouth, but he will soon do so if you place your first finger between his lips on the off-side until you can slide it into the gap where he has no teeth. You should be able to find this gap quite easily.

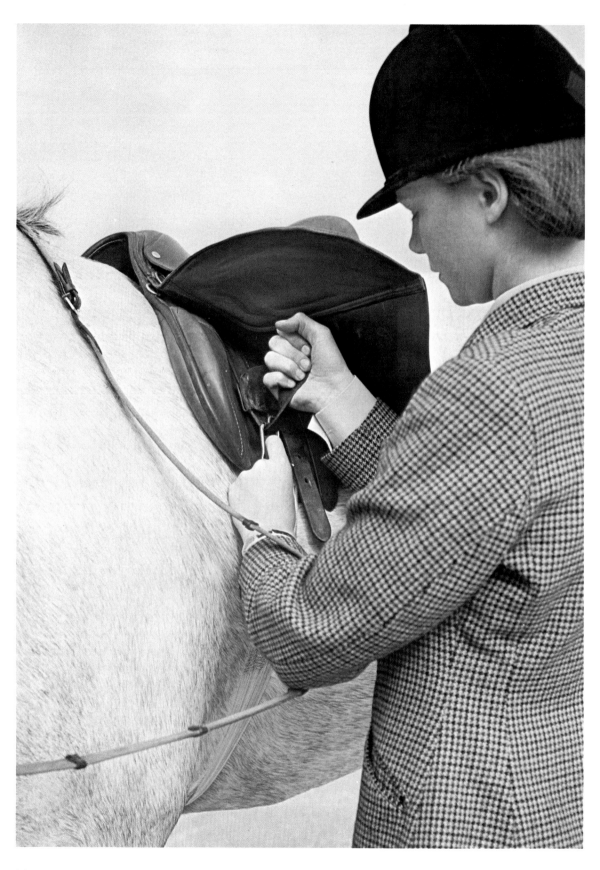

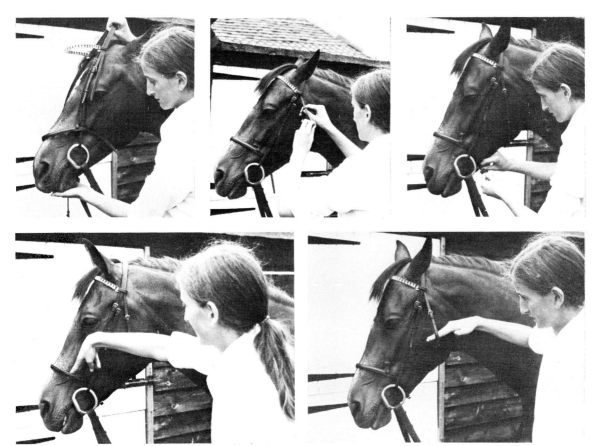

Putting on a bridle
Top, left: slipping the bit into the mouth; *top, centre:* tightening-up the throat lash; *top, right:* doing up the noseband; *above, left:* checking the noseband; *above right:* checking the throat lash

Left: before mounting the rider tightens the girth while still having the reins linked through the arm

While you have been doing this your right hand should have been holding the headpiece close to his forehead, so that you will now be able to draw the bridle up over his head, and use your left hand to guide the bit into his mouth.

Once the bit is safely in a pony's mouth you will have both hands free to put the headpiece over each ear in turn. Never pull or jolt the bit into his mouth. Doing so will only make a pony more difficult on the next occasion.

Smooth down the mane and pull the forelock over the brow-band. Then run your fingers round under the headpiece to make sure that nothing is twisted and that the hair is lying correctly.

You will now be ready to do up the loose straps and run the ends through their keepers and runners. Start from the top of the bridle and work downwards, making sure that the nose band is inside the cheek pieces on both sides.

Finally, walk round to the pony's head to make certain that the brow-band is level, just below the ears but not touching them, and that the bridle is on straight with the holes in the cheek pieces level.

You should be able to get two fingers between the front of the pony's face and the nose-band, and the full width of your hand between the throat lash and his jaw bone.

If you are not going to use the pony immediately, leave the

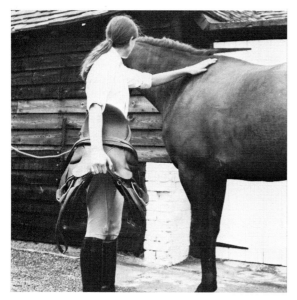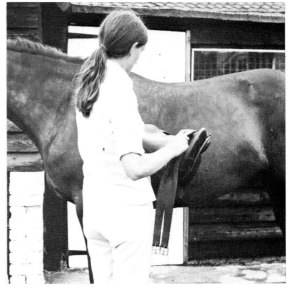

stırrups up on the saddle, and slide the ends of the reins under-neath them in order to prevent him from rolling or putting his head down and pulling the reins over his head, where they can become trodden on and broken.

Some people–when they are putting on a bridle–prefer to put their right hand under a pony's jaw and up round his face just above his nostrils. Then, holding both cheek pieces in their right hand, they again use their left hand to open the pony's mouth and guide in the bit.

Both methods are correct. The second method probably gives a little more control in steadying the pony's head and preventing any sideways movement.

Taking off the saddle and bridle is quite simple. Starting with the saddle, run the irons up the stirrup leathers and tuck the ends of the loops through the irons to hold them in place. Take the reins over the pony's head and slip the ends into the crook of your arm nearest his head. Raise the saddle flap and undo the buckle of the girth, letting the end hang loose. If the pony is wearing a martingale, slip the loop from the girth and then, with one hand on the front arch of the saddle and the other on the cantle, or rear part of the seat, slide the saddle off the pony's back, on to your forearm so that the front arch rests in the crook of your elbow.

Next slide the girth, dirty side upwards, over the seat of the saddle, and place it down somewhere safe where it will not get knocked over or damaged.

Run your hands over the pony's back to make sure that there are not any lumps, and look under his belly to make sure that the girth has not rubbed any sore patches–known as girth galls. Then pat briskly the area where the saddle has been to help dry any sweaty patches and restore the circulation.

Putting on and taking off a saddle
Above, left: approach quietly from the near-side
Above, right: the saddle, with girth attachcd is hcld ovcr thc left arm

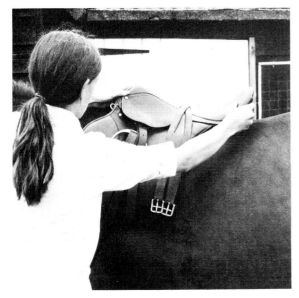

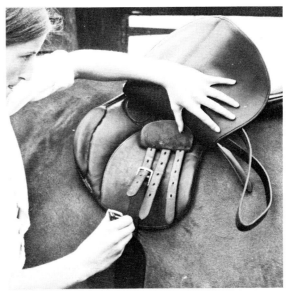

Above, left: place the saddle gently on the pony's back. Slide it into position
Above, right: doing up the girth

Now move round to the bridle, first making sure that you have a headcollar or halter ready to secure the pony with when the bridle has been removed. Put your arm through the headcollar and let it rest on your shoulder out of the way, while you put the reins back over the pony's neck. This will give you something to hold on to and also with which to control the pony if he decides to try and move away.

In undoing the bridle remember that the opposite to putting on a bridle applies. You start at the mouth upwards, so that you begin with the curb chain, if the pony is wearing one, then undo the nose band followed by the throat lash.

When the straps of the nose band and the throat lash have been undone, place your left hand on the pony's face just above his nostrils, and use your right hand to slip the headpiece over his ears so that it can slide down on to your left forearm. Always ease the bit out of the pony's mouth. Never let it drop out suddenly or he may throw his head back and hurt his mouth. For the same reason any curb chain must be undone first.

Then slip the whole bridle, with the exception of the reins, on to your left shoulder, so that it is out of the way and you have both hands free to put the headcollar over the pony's head, and do up the strap before slipping the reins over his head.

Tie-up the pony securely and check that the bit has not rubbed his mouth. If he seems cold, put his ears gently between your thumb and fingers until they feel warm and dry.

Next, keeping the bridle, and martingale if there is one, over your left shoulder, pick up the saddle and girth and, holding the saddle with the front arch in the crook of your arm or along your thigh if you find this easier, take them to the tack room ready to be cleaned.

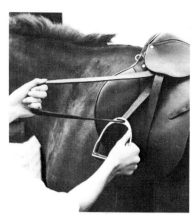

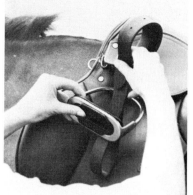

Above, left: before unsaddling, the stirrup irons should be run-up through the leathers; *centre:* and made secure by tucking the leathers through the stirrups; *right:* this will prevent the stirrups from sliding down the leathers when the saddle is being carried from the pony

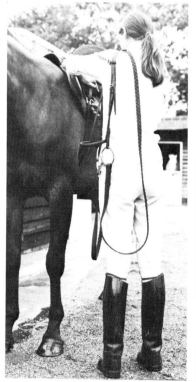

Above: the bridle can be placed over the shoulder, leaving both hands free to take off the saddle

Below: the bit should carefully be slipped out of the pony's mouth

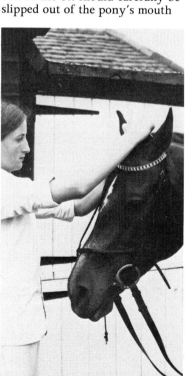

Above: as the saddle is removed the girth is placed across the seat

10

Mounting and dismounting

Now that the time has arrived for you to get into the saddle and start to ride, clothing becomes important. We will be dealing in a later chapter with the clothes you will need for riding in competitions, but to start with you will only require enough for your own safety.

The four main articles of clothing are a hard riding hat, a pair of jodhpurs or strong jeans to protect your legs from becoming sore, a jacket or a good, long-sleeved sweater to protect your arms, and strong boots or shoes (with a heel) to prevent your feet from slipping through the stirrup irons.

Never get on a horse or pony unless you are wearing a hard hat and shoes with a heel, even if you are only planning to walk round the stable yard. Many riders have been injured unnecessarily because they ignored this basic commonsense rule.

Ponies cannot always be relied upon to stand quietly while their rider climbs into the saddle, and it is consequently important for you to learn to mount in such a way that you will be able to swing yourself up into the saddle without getting left behind if a pony suddenly moves.

Because cowboys ride in saddles with high pommels they have to mount facing a horse's head. With a European type of saddle the reverse is, however, the case. Always stand ready to mount with your shoulder alongside the pony's shoulder, facing his tail. To begin with it is easier to learn to mount from the near side, but as you become more experienced you should be able to get on to your pony from either side.

Before getting into the saddle it is as well to check that your stirrup leathers are the correct length, so that once you are mounted you will be able to put your feet home in the stirrups and be ready for any move a pony may make. Do this by standing facing the saddle and pulling the stirrup irons down to the bottom of the leathers. Then clench your fist and place the knuckles of your right hand on the stirrup bar of the saddle. With your left hand hold the stirrup leather and iron up to your right arm-pit. If the leathers are the correct length the stirrup iron should just reach into your arm-pit. Although some people

Checking the length of stirrup
leathers before mounting

like to ride longer or shorter than others, this is still a very good
way of judging the correct length while you are on the ground.

Having made sure that your stirrup irons are down and the
leathers are correct, lift the saddle flap and check that the girth
is tight enough to prevent the saddle from slipping when you
put your weight in the stirrup. While you are doing this it is as
well to see that the girth is not pinching any part of a pony's skin
and that the buckle guards are in place to protect the buckles.
You will probably have to put the girths up another hole once
you are in the saddle, so leave some spare holes free under the
buckle guard.

When you are ready to mount, stand with your left shoulder
alongside the pony's near shoulder, and take the reins and stick
in your left hand. The reins should be short enough for you to
control the pony if he moves forward, separated ready for riding
with the off-side rein slightly shorter than the near side. In this
way, if he moves the reins will steer him to the right, and his
body will be brought round towards you, making it easier for
you to get your right leg across the saddle.

Place your left hand holding the reins in front of the withers.
When they are learning some people also like to take a grip of the
mane. Then, holding the iron steady with the right hand, put
your left foot into the stirrup. Press down the toes under the
girth, and pivot your body round until you are facing the pony.
Put across your right hand until you can seize the waist of the

Neatly illustrated is the way to
mount and dismount

saddle on the far side and spring lightly upwards. As you do so, swing your right leg over the pony's back – taking care that your foot does not give him a bang on his quarters and cause him to jump forward. As your leg comes over, move your right hand to the front of the pommel and allow your body to sink gently into the saddle. You will then be able to place your right foot quietly into the stirrup iron, and have your pony under control.

Once you are safely in the saddle it is important to check your girth once again, and it may also be necessary to make some alteration to the length of your stirrup irons. Whether you are altering your girths or your stirrup leathers, you should never take your foot out of the stirrups. To deal with the girth, put the reins in one hand and bring your off-side knee forward until you can lift the saddle flap. Check the girth with your fingers, and if it needs tightening take each girth strap in turn and, having first loosened the buckle, pull it up a hole using your first finger to guide it into place. When both buckles are securely in position pull down the buckle guard and let the saddle flap fall back into place. You will then be able to take up your correct position in the saddle.

Altering the length of the stirrups is also quite easy. To change the left stirrup, put the reins in the right hand, and take hold of the spare end of the stirrup leather with the left. By placing your thumb on top of the buckle, steer the tongue of the buckle with your first finger using the other three fingers to hold the spare end of the leather. As soon as the tongue becomes disengaged guide it into the correct hole. Then move the buckle until it fits snugly against the bar of the saddle by pulling down on the inside leather, and pressing down the stirrup iron. You should get into the habit of being able to alter the length of your stirrups from the saddle without looking down.

When you want to dismount, remember that you must first of all remove both your feet from the stirrups. Only when using a Western saddle would one dismount with a foot in the stirrup.

After ensuring that both feet are clear of the stirrup irons, lean forward and place your left hand, which should also be holding the stick, on the pony's neck. Then, placing your right hand on the pommel of the saddle, bend your right knee and vault off, making sure that you do not kick the pony as you bring your right leg over his back. Land gently on your toes, clear of your pony's front legs, and you will then be able to use your right hand to take a firm hold of the reins close up to the bit.

You will no doubt have seen some riders dismounting by throwing their leg over their pony's withers and sliding to the ground. This may look clever, but it is really very foolish because in doing so they have to let go of the reins and lose control of their pony, with the result that if he does move suddenly they can take a nasty fall.

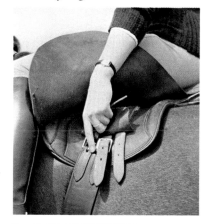

Once in the saddle the girths should again be checked and, if necessary, tightened

The feet should be kept in the stirrup irons while the leathers are adjusted

11

Sitting correctly

Your seat on a horse or pony is important – not only because of the way you look but also because of the control a good seat will give you over an animal's movements.

Good horsemen ride most of the time by balance and poise, and they keep their position by a combination of balance, suppleness and grip. They sit in the centre and lowest part of the saddle and, although remaining supple, are always in a position to grip quickly when they feel themselves becoming unbalanced.

The first essential for any rider is to acquire a good, strong seat which is completely independent of the reins. Regular practice will help, but the correct length of stirrup leather is important. Beginners frequently ride with their stirrups too short. If you practice riding for a while without stirrups – stretching your legs and toes as far as they will go – you will find that you will be able to get lower in the saddle, and probably need to lengthen your leathers when you start riding with stirrups once again.

As you start to get the feel of a pony you should begin to develop a firm seat well down in the saddle. The upper part of your body should be upright, but it must always remain supple, particularly at the waist, because stiffness in one part of the body will quickly produce muscular contractions in another. Your head should be erect with the shoulders square so that you can look straight between the pony's ears.

Keep your knees and thighs close to the saddle. Learning the correct position will enable you to develop a natural grip downwards and inwards. Your knees and ankles must remain supple because stiffness in these joints will also cause stiffness in the upper part of your body.

The lower part of your legs should be kept slightly behind the girth so that they can be used to apply the aids without any sudden movement. If your legs are in the correct position the stirrup leathers will be perpendicular to the ground. It is particularly important to develop a correct position for the lower part of your legs because an incorrect one will only create bad balance.

Right: riding without stirrups helps the rider to get lower in the saddle

94

Above: the rider demonstrates how a single rein is passed round the little finger and held in place by the thumb and first finger

Holding double reins while carrying a stick

Your heels should be below the level of your toes to enable the important muscles on the inside of your thighs to remain taut, and your knees to be low on the saddle. Keep your knees and toes pointing towards the front. Turning out your toes will tend to make you grip with the back of your calfs.

The stirrups should be held on the ball of your foot so that your ankle can remain supple. You can always thrust your feet home in the stirrups when necessary.

Let your arms hang naturally down to the elbows, lightly touching your hips. Your forearms should form a straight line along the reins to the pony's mouth. Keep your hands just above and in front of the saddle, with the thumbs upwards and your wrists and fingers supple enough to be able to follow the movements of the pony's head and neck.

The reins should normally be held in both hands but there will be occasions when you will need only to hold them in one hand. If you are using a snaffle or single-rein bridle and you want to hold both reins in your left hand, take the right rein between either the first and second fingers or the first finger and thumb. The left rein should then be held outside the fourth finger with the slack part of the reins across the palm of your left hand.

To hold the reins in both hands, place your right hand on the right rein with the rein outside your little finger and take it from the left hand. Let the slack part of the reins pass between the finger and thumb of each hand. Some riders, however, prefer to hold the reins between the little finger and the third finger because they feel it gives them a better grip.

If your pony is wearing a double bridle with two reins, these can be held in the left hand by placing your little finger between the two left reins and your second finger between the two right reins. The slack of the reins can then pass between your first finger and thumb.

To take the reins in both hands, divide them with the little finger of each hand with the bridoon or snaffle rein on the outside.

12

The 'aids'—the rider's signalling system

A rider conveys his intentions to his pony by way of 'aids', and these are the universal signals which you and your pony must learn to understand. They must be given clearly and accurately, so that he will change pace or direction smoothly.

The term 'aids' not only refers to the signals you give to indicate your wishes, but also to the means at your disposal for making the signals.

There are *natural* aids, given by the hands, legs, body and voice, and *artificial* aids—where the rider uses a stick, spurs and items of saddlery, like a martingale.

When learning you should concentrate on the natural aids, starting with the body and making full use of the back muscles and seat. By bracing the back muscles you can then straighten your spine—pushing forwards and downwards through the seat, knees and heels.

The legs can then be used to increase pace and energy by pressing the thighs and the inside of the calves against the horse's side. When this is done the toes should only be turned slightly outwards, making sure that the heels are not dug into the horse's ribs.

As a means of controlling the hindquarters, remember your legs can either be used separately or together in partnership with the hands.

Through the reins, the hands can either regulate the energy created by the legs, control the horse's forehand, or guide and alter his rhythm and pace.

The voice is an aid which many novice riders only remember in an emergency. It should, however, be used to encourage, soothe or to check a movement. It is also effective as a means of frightening a horse into obeying an important command.

One aid, however, is of little use without the other. They should be used together.

Artificial aids must be used carefully and only when a rider is fully aware of their correct use.

A stick or cane looks correct and is easiest to handle when about one quarter protrudes in front of the hand, and points in

Above: the horse's hindquarters are controlled by the legs being used in partnership with the hands
Above, right: a stick or cane should point in the direction of the horse's opposite ear

the direction of the horse's opposite ear. You should practice changing the stick quickly and smoothly from one hand to the other. Being able to do this efficiently is important when schooling a horse over jumps or when a horse shies at an obstacle which has to be passed. It should be used just behind your leg, and only when the horse fails to respond to your legs.

The hunting whip – which must always have a thong and lash – is carried in the same way as a stick – with the hook to the rear, pointing towards the ground. It is useful for opening gates, or for keeping hounds away from a horse's legs by holding it outwards so that the thong and lash hang downwards.

Spurs should never be used as a method of punishment. They are purely an aid to make a horse lighter and more responsive to the legs. In the early stages of learning to ride spurs should not be worn. Later, with more experience and understanding, they should be applied gently, with the inside of the spur against the horse's side. Remember your toes must not be turned outward, or the back of the spurs will be brought into contact with the horse with very unpleasant results.

Learning to apply the aids correctly will take time. It will require a knowledge of technique as well as some natural ability. To get the best results the signals given to a horse must be light but positive. With a well-trained animal they should be given in such a way that they are very difficult for an onlooker to discern.

13

Moving through the paces

Once you know how to signal your intentions to your horse or pony in a way in which he will understand, you should be able to move smoothly through the paces from a walk to a trot, and then on to a canter and gallop, and finally back to a halt.

When you want a pony to walk forwards, squeeze slightly behind the girth with your legs and urge him on with your seat and back while at the same time keeping a light contact with his mouth. To achieve the best results you will need to gain complete harmony between your body, legs and hands.

As a pony walks forward, do not alter the position of your body, but look ahead in the direction in which you are going and move in rhythm with the natural movement of the pony.

To move from the walk to the trot, sit down in the saddle and use the same instructions or aids as you would to change from the halt to the walk.

There are two ways of riding at the trot. There is the 'sitting trot'–when your seat remains in the saddle–and the 'rising trot' when you rise in time with the motion of the pony. A horse or pony trots in two-time with the off-fore and the near-hindleg going together, and the near-fore and the off-hindleg on the same diagonal. You will be said to be riding on the right diagonal when your seat returns to the saddle as a pony's off-fore and near-hindleg touch the ground together. You can 'change' the diagonal by sitting down in the saddle for an extra beat before starting to rise again.

The rising trot should be an easy motion for you and a pony without any jerks or bumps. Incline the upper part of your body forward slightly and keep the small of your back supple. Do not make an effort to rise in the saddle, but let the pony do all the work, leaving you to take the weight on your knee and ankle joints. If your back is stiff and hollow your stomach will be pushed forward as your rise, and there will be a tendency for you to pull yourself up with the reins. Practice will enable you to trot easily and without any noticeable exertion.

By sitting down and keeping a light contact with the pony's mouth you will be able to use your legs to squeeze him forward into a canter.

Cantering disunited

Cantering united

A pony will be said to be cantering 'true' or 'united' when his leading foreleg and leading hindleg appear both to be on the same side. He will be cantering 'disunited' when his leading hindleg appears to be on the opposite side to his leading foreleg.

Remember that the pace of the canter is three-time so that there are three distinct beats to each stride. The upper part of your body should give in time with the rhythm and motion of the pony, and your seat should remain close to the saddle. It may sound difficult, but you will soon learn to go with your pony.

If your back is stiff and rigid you will bump up and down in the saddle. Getting your weight too far forward off the bones of your bottom is another common fault which must be mastered.

When you have learnt to sit easily at the canter you should learn to make the pony strike off with the correct leg.

If you are going to canter to the left the pony should lead with his near-foreleg, and if you are cantering to the right he should lead with his off-fore.

To make him lead with his off-fore, put the pony into a trot and flex him slightly to the right with your right rein, sitting well down in the saddle as you do so. Then squeeze with both legs, keeping your left leg a little further back than your right. The object of keeping your left leg behind the girth is to prevent the pony's quarters from swinging out and also to let him know exactly what is required of him.

To canter with the near-fore leading, reverse the process so that you flex the pony to the left with your left rein, and sitting well-down in the saddle, squeeze with your right leg behind the girth.

From the canter you can use your legs in conjunction with your hands to urge the pony on into a gallop. Either sit well down in the saddle and drive the pony forward with your seat and legs, or adopt a forward position so that the weight of your body is taken on your knees and stirrups. Your seat should be off the saddle, with your body leaning forward over your hands, and your weight poised over the centre of gravity.

It is easy to maintain this position providing you keep a firm and even contact with the pony through the bit.

You should remember that your hands must be sensitive to every reaction in the pony's mouth. They should always be used in conjunction with your legs and back, and be held at waist height on either side of the pony's withers. When you want the pony to slow down, close both your legs into his sides, straighten your spine and drive him up into what is termed a 'resisting' hand. Your pony should decrease pace smoothly and hold his head steady. When he halts he should be made to stand squarely on all four legs. As soon as he has obeyed your command, relax both your legs and the pressure on the reins.

There will be occasions when you will want the pony to rein-back. Before asking him to do so make sure that he is standing straight, with his jaw relaxed, and his head held fairly low.

Push him up into his bit by pressure from your legs and seat, but instead of yielding with your hands, as you would if you wanted him to walk forward, retain the pressure on the reins. The pony should rein-back in two-time and move in a straight line. As soon as he has taken the necessary number of steps backwards ease the reins and allow him to come to a halt, before going forward once more.

Reining back – see foot of page 102

14

An approach to jumping

After you have mastered the aids and feel secure and confident at a walk, trot, canter and gallop, you will probably want to move on to jumping.

The art of jumping is not as difficult as it sounds, providing you adopt the correct position and learn to go with your horse or pony without interfering with his freedom of action over a jump.

Watch a horse taking an obstacle without a rider on his back. As he approaches the jump he lowers his head, and stretches out his neck, so that he can balance himself ready to take the leap forward and upwards. At the moment of take-off he shortens his neck which slightly raises his head and enables him to lift up his forehand. As his hocks come underneath him, he stretches his head and neck once again and makes a spring upwards and forwards. He gathers his hind legs under his belly as he goes over the obstacle, and then as he lands his head comes up and his neck shortens.

The rider has to learn to 'go with' the horse so that he does not hinder the freedom of action, or jab his mount in the mouth, which would dissuade him from jumping with any enthusiasm in the future.

Before jumping, many riders find it easier if they shorten their stirrup leathers a hole or so, although when they do so it is important that they should avoid any tendency to stand up in the stirrups when they are jumping, by straightening their knees.

When taking up the jumping position you should always be looking in the direction of the fence with your head up and body as still as possible. Your back should be straight and supple, with the shoulders forward and the weight taken on knees and thighs. Your heels should be pressed down with the seat close to the saddle.

Your arms must not be pushed out sideways but be slightly bent at the elbow – so that they form a straight line from the elbow through the forearms, hands and reins to the horse's mouth and bit.

Shoulders, arms and fingers must be supple enough to follow

the movements of the horse's head and yet maintain a good 'feel' or contact, without interfering with the horse's natural jumping action.

The soles of your feet must be far enough home in the stirrups to keep them firm, with the heels lower than the toes, enabling the ankles to be flexible and act as shock absorbers. Your lower legs should be kept close to the sides of the horse in order that the stirrup leathers can remain perpendicular to the ground.

Horses do not always jump confidently – and you must keep a supple waist so that you will be ready to respond to any last minute check in a horse's rhythm, particularly if you feel that a horse is going to make an awkward take-off.

As the horse rises at an obstacle, you should feel close to the saddle, maintain the correct jumping position by a combination of balance and grip, while following the movements of the horse.

Your weight should be kept away from the loins, and your hands and arms should follow the lengthening and shortening of the horse or pony's head without losing steady contact with the mouth.

The jumping position, because it allows you to follow the horse's movements, and use your thighs, knees and ankle joints as shock absorbers, is also the position to adopt when negotiating steep slopes and hills.

Right: clearing a cross-country obstacle

Above and right: three different types of obstacle found in the show jumping ring

Riding down a bank

Horses usually jump badly because of bad schooling or bad riding, and for this reason it is important for you to learn to present a horse at a fence correctly and have the necessary knowledge and determination to get him to jump enthusiastically and well.

When learning to jump it is a good idea to practice over cavalletti. In this way you will develop the correct position over a fence and be able to combine suppleness, balance, strength and style. It will also help you to get used to the rhythm of a horse or pony when approaching and taking-off over an obstacle, and to learn to judge his stride.

This style of training will additionally help to develop a horse's muscles, balance, suppleness and agility, while at the same time teaching him obedience and calmness.

Cavalletti jumps are poles approximately 3 m (9·9 ft) and fixed to wooden cross pieces so that they may be placed either 25 cm (10 ins), 36 cm (15 ins), or 50 cm (19 ins) from the ground.

The best way is to start with a single cavalletti in the lowest position and allow the horse to walk over it. Then approach the pole with more impulsion at a trot. When you and your horse or pony are happily negotiating a single cavalletti, more can be added. These should be placed approximately 1·22 m (4 ft) or 1·52 m (5 ft) apart, according to the stride.

You should be able to negotiate half a dozen cavalletti at a trot with a smooth regular rhythm so that you are supple and there is no discomfort to the horse. When the horse is trotting, the poles should only be 25 cm (10 ins) in height.

A small jump can then be introduced by placing two cavalletti together. The jump may gradually be widened and increased in height by the use of other cavalletti.

After you are confidently jumping two or more cavalletti from a trot, it will be time to do the same exercise at a canter. When doing this, a pole on the ground may be used as a distance guide to show the horse when to take off, so that by preventing him from getting too close to the obstacle, you will find the jump easier.

Because horses sometimes get excited when jumping – and this can be unsettling for the novice – practice fences should not be placed in a straight line. It is much better if they are jumped in a sequence which allows changes of rein. This will help quieten down the horse and give you a better opportunity of keeping control.

Never try to jump too high too quickly. Keep the jumps low – until you have confidence and can adapt yourself to any sudden alteration of stride or hesitation when approaching a jump. It is usually better to increase the spread rather than the height.

Jumping the larger obstacles will come quite easily and naturally once you can cope with smaller obstacles with the correct flexibility and timing.

Schooling ponies over coloured
poles laid on the ground

Below: riding through a line of
cavalletti

A single cavalletto

Cavalletti forming a spread

Below: approaching a practice jump under the eye of an instructor

15

Clipping and trimming

Every horse or pony required to carry out fast work during the winter, when his coat is heavy, needs to be clipped, but the extent of the clip will depend on the type of work and also whether the animal is being stabled. If the hair is left long, the animal will only sweat up and lose condition.

There is an old saying that riding an unclipped horse is like being expected to race in an overcoat.

A horse turned out with a New Zealand rug will usually require a **Trace clip** or blanket clip. In the case of the trace clip, which was very popular for harness horses some years ago, the hair is removed from the under-surface of the body and along the windpipe area of the neck. In some cases a narrow line is also run up the quarters to the tail. The hair is left long on the legs and back, but there are three variations of the clip—high, medium and low—according to how high the hair is left on the sides. The **Blanket clip** is similar, but the hair on the neck and head is removed and cut square where a blanket usually lies across the withers and shoulders.

A stabled hunter should be fully clipped out with the exception of his legs, the triangle at the top of the tail, and the saddle patch. This is known as the **Hunter clip** and the hair on the legs is left long as a protection against injuries from thorns—as well as cracked heels and mud fever. The saddle patch is left to absorb some of the sweat and to alleviate pressure and chafing.

Alternatively, horses can be given the **Full clip** when they are clipped right out—with the exception of the triangle above the tail.

There is another type of clip sometimes seen on the race-course known as the **Chaser clip**—when all the hair is removed from the head, and the lower part of the neck and body up the sides to the area where the saddle flaps would be. The hair on the top part of the body—from behind the ears on the neck through to the tail—is left long to provide protection. Sometimes the clip is taken up the quarters and rounded-off, making it look very smart and workmanlike.

Undoubtedly clipping makes a great difference to a horse's appearance. It also makes it very much easier for him to be kept

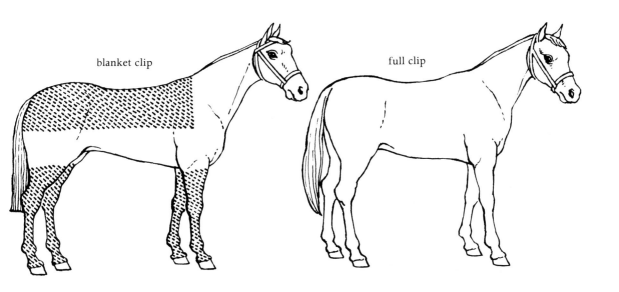

blanket clip

full clip

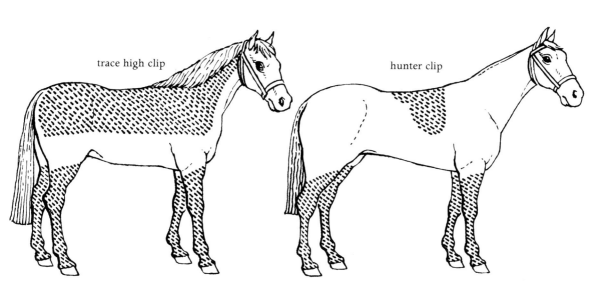

trace high clip

hunter clip

clean and tidy. Horses or ponies should get their first clip of the season in late autumn. They usually start to grow their winter coats at the end of the summer when the coat begins to look dull and rough – and it should then be left until the winter coat becomes properly established (about a month to six weeks later), before any of it is removed.

In the case of horses which have been clipped right out, it is quite usual to leave the legs and saddle patch on with the second clip. This makes them look less hairy than they would if their legs had been left unclipped in the autumn. The positioning of the saddle patch can alter the appearance of an animal. Care should consequently be taken to ensure that the patch is in the right place and also clipped round evenly. One way of doing this is to clip round a numnah. Always remember that a clipped-out horse will feel the cold at exercise early in the morning, with the result that he may well be inclined to buck and play about. A fresh horse and sleepy rider can be soon parted!

In mid-winter a horse can be given a light clip to remove any 'cat' hairs which otherwise look so long, coarse and unsightly, as well as collecting mud. If the animal has a coarse coat it is far better to clip fairly frequently, than to clip too close the first time and cause him to feel cold. Horses do not like shocks to their systems any more than humans do, and they should never be clipped if the weather is very wet or frosty or if there is a cold wind. A cold horse will never be a contented horse.

Clipping is an art which can be acquired quite easily providing you follow some simple rules. The first rule is *never* be in a hurry. If you make a mistake you cannot put back the hair . . . and many a trace-clip has ended as a full-clip because the groom was trying to go too quickly. Make sure that your equipment is working properly, and you have a spare set of sharp blades in case a tooth becomes broken, or the pair already in the clippers became blunt. You should, in any case, have the coarser pair of blades needed for the legs.

There are two types of electric clipper. There is the lighter hand-type with the motor in the handle – easy to use and which will be perfectly adequate providing you do not allow them to become overheated, and your horse has a normal coat which is not too thick. The alternative is the heavy duty-type normally used in the larger professional stables where the clippers are in more frequent use. This has a powerful clipper which hangs from a wall bracket and has a flexible shaft to which the cutting head is attached.

Whichever machine you use, remember to maintain it properly, and follow a few commonsense rules to ensure that it is only asked to function under the circumstances for which it was designed. Properly-serviced electric clipping machines rarely give trouble, but any that are neglected usually become a constant nuisance.

Before starting, make sure that your horse or pony is as dry and as clean as his coat will permit. Tie him up with a halter attached to a loop of string fastened to the ring. If you are clipping him in his box, stack his bed along the walls, and sweep the centre of the floor clean and dry. It is important to remember that you are using an electric appliance, so that if your horse has steel shoes on a wet floor, and your clippers develop a fault, there is a risk of electrocution.

It is best always to wear rubber boots or rubber-soled shoes when clipping. If you feel the clippers vibrate or if they give off

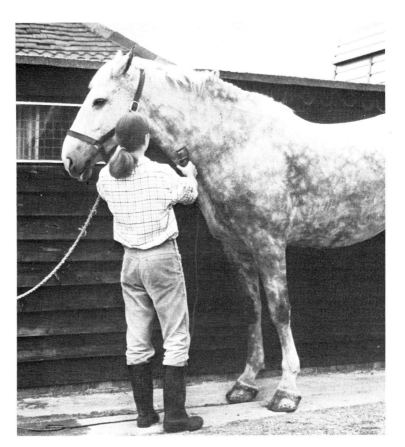

When clipping you should wear rubber boots and keep the electric lead away from the horse's feet. In cold weather a blanket should be used to keep the horse warm

any shock, turn them off immediately at the mains switch, and don't use them again until the fault has been properly diagnosed and repaired.

You will not want your animal's hair to get in the way while you are working, and so before you clip plait up the mane with elastic bands, and double the tail up and enclose it in a tail bandage. Remember that it is easy to catch the mane or tail in the clippers and they need to be kept out of the way. Place a folded rug over the horse's back before starting—because a cold horse will be a fidgety horse and make clipping that much more difficult. Make sure he has a full haynet to keep him amused while you get on with the job.

When you plug into the socket and switch on at the mains, stand well back from your horse before switching on the clippers. Let them run free for a few moments so that he can get used to the noise—and you can ensure that they are running smoothly. Then, adjust the tension screw by turning it until the clipper speed slows down. Next, turn it up about half a turn to let it return to its normal speed, and run an oil can containing thin oil along the blades and in the oil holes. If the blades are too tight, the engine will be strained and become overheated. When you are satisfied that everything is in order, start on the hindquarters—keeping the blades running into the coat in the direction that it is growing and keep them at an angle, with the points slightly upwards so that they glide smoothly over his skin.

The height of the hair on the legs—unless you are clipping right out—is a matter of preference, but it is usual to clip the fore legs from the elbow to the natural groove by the chest, and from the stifle (or just below) to a point about a hand's width above the hocks on the hind legs. You must get both sides even, working a little on one side and then moving over to the other. If you are trace clipping, lift the clippers to make a straight edge, and do not try to take the coat line too high all at once. Keep below the line you are aiming at to begin with—until you are sure that you have the correct height and that both sides will match. Move the rug as you work to make sure your horse does not get cold. Remember to let the machine do the work so that all you have to do is guide the blades, and make sure that the coat line remains level.

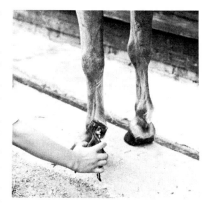

Brush the coat regularly to remove the loose hairs. If you feel that the clippers are getting too hot, switch them off for a while. Use the time that they are cooling down to clear the hair out of the blades and re-oil them.

When it comes to doing the head and neck, slip the halter round his neck so that you are free to hold his head still with one hand while you use the clippers with the other. If a horse starts to play up, take your time doing his head, and if he refuses to settle down it is much better to use a twitch than to have a battle which you will almost certainly lose. A horse which is really hard to clip may need a veterinary surgeon to give him a tranquilliser. If you have to use what is known as a twitch, it should be placed on the nose below the nostrils, and held steady by a helper. Never ever use a twitch on the ear. To do so is cruel, and will make the horse much worse in the long run.

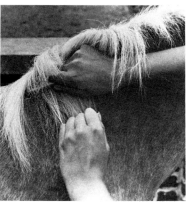

Top: trimming the heels
Above: pulling the mane

Never clip the hair from inside the ears or interfere with the long hair in the muzzle area. Care must be taken not to clip the mane or tail, and the clippers should not be used on the back of the tendons or fetlocks. If the hair will not pull easily, use scissors and a comb—moving them upwards against the hair.

Heels can be trimmed with a comb and scissors or with a pair of hand clippers. These can also be used to take away the long coarse 'cat' hairs in the region of the jaw, between the chin groove and the throat.

After you have finished clipping, and checked that both sides are the same, brush the coat thoroughly to remove any remaining loose hairs, unplait the mane, and take off the tail bandages before putting the rug straight. When you have made the horse comfortable, brush the stable floor, and give him an extra depth of bedding to help keep him warm. Then clean the clippers thoroughly before oiling them and putting them away ready for use next time.

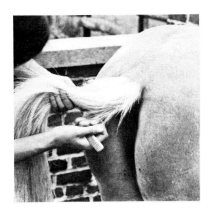

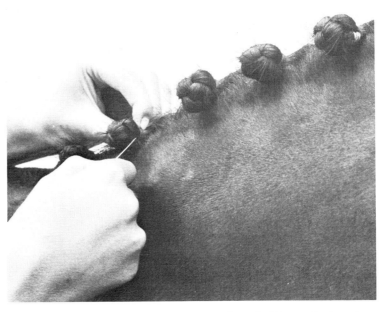

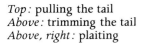
Top: pulling the tail
Above: trimming the tail
Above, right: plaiting

After a horse has been clipped he will probably need trimming. The mane, tail, jaw, ears and heels will all need trimming from time to time. Manes should always be pulled or hogged. Pulling is done – either to thin out a mane which is too thick and long or to make it lie flat. The longest hairs underneath should be removed, a few at a time, by winding them round a finger and giving a short, sharp pull. Never pull the top hairs, and on no account use the scissors or clippers for this purpose. You will need a brush to get rid of any tangles, and a comb to get the mane lying straight on its natural side. Work up the neck – from the withers and then down again. Do a little at a time. If you remove too much you will only make the crest sore.

The length of the tail is usually a matter of preference, but a tail that is too long can hamper a horse, particularly when jumping, and it is usual to square-off the tail so that the end reaches somewhere between the hocks and the fetlocks. A swish tail is one which is allowed to come to a point, by brushing out the bottom until it becomes wispy. The top of the tail in the dock region can either be left long, so that it may be plaited, or it can be pulled a little at a time. To pull a tail, first brush it straight with a body brush and remove all the tangles. Then, starting at the sides, take one or two hairs between your first finger and thumb, and slide the trimming comb up the other hairs so that those to be removed are uncovered. Then pass the centre finger over the

hairs and, pressing down firmly with the comb, pull them out gently by the roots. Keep both sides even by taking out a few hairs at a time. The secret is to do it slowly, little by little. When the tail has been finished, a tail bandage should be put in place. If a horse is inclined to kick, tie him up so that his tail falls over the stable door or, better still, use a straw bale for protection. The process should not be painful to the horse. If it is you are either taking too many hairs at a time, or you are trying to do the job too quickly. The hairs of the mane and the tail will pull more easily when the pores of the skin are warm and open when he returns from exercise, or when the weather is warm.

Manes are plaited for neatness, to show off the neck and crest, and to train the hair to fall into place on the correct side, which is normally the off side. It is usual to have an odd number of plaits along the neck, and one on the forelock.

When a horse is hogged all the hairs of the mane are removed with the clippers. It can only be done properly when someone stands in front of the horse and gently forces his head down by taking hold of the ears so that the crest is stretched. Starting at the withers and working towards the poll, the whole of the mane is taken off, making sure that no unsightly line is left where the coat and crest meet. Hogging needs to be done about every three weeks, and once a mane has been hogged it will usually take at least two years to grow properly.

When the time comes to turn out a horse that has been clipped during the winter months, remember that he will have to be roughed off to prepare him for the change in environment and diet. This will usually take about two weeks. During that period his ration of concentrates needs to be reduced gradually, and fast work should stop so that his exercise is restricted to walking

A well turned out pony and rider

and trotting. The blankets should gradually be discarded, and he should be stabled at night without rugs for about a week before being turned out completely. The best time to do this is in early summer, preferably when the weather is mild and dry.

There are electrically operated grooming machines, which are especially useful in stables where there are a number of horses to do and when labour is short. They have a massaging effect, and are quite efficient at removing dirt and grease as well as putting a final polish to the coat. The tail, however, should be tied out of the way, and you should wear a hat or headscarf, for the sake of safety, if your hair is long.

16

The horse's feet

There is a well-known saying 'No foot, no horse'– and how true that is! Do not forget that the few square inches which go to make up the foot of a horse or pony have to support not only his own weight, and absorb the strain and concussion of galloping and jumping on various types of ground, but also the weight of a rider who may not always be in the correct place at the right time! Nature never intended them to have to do that. Remember that when a horse is galloping or jumping he brings one fore foot down to the ground at a time, with the result that more than half a ton is forced down on one small area. When this is borne in mind, it is quite remarkable that horses do not get more foot trouble.

Severe concussion or strain can cause inflammation. In other parts of the body this would show as a swelling – because nature would rush an extra lot of blood to the affected area to help it to heal. In the case of a horse's foot, however, the damaged part is prevented from swelling by the box-like nature of the hoof. This can lead to all sorts of complications until eventually the bones may become displaced, or deformed unless the trouble is treated properly. Even so some lameness in the foot cannot be dealt with effectively because it is not possible to reach the injured areas of inflammation and poison.

When you next pick up a horse's hoof, take a good look at the way in which it has been formed. Make sure you know the correct names of the various parts, so that you can describe them properly if you need to do so. The horse's foot is a highly sensitive organ inside its outer wall, and it can be easily damaged – a fact which many people unfortunately forget.

The size and shape of the foot will vary from horse to horse. Some are broad and round, while others are long and narrow, but a good-shaped foot is something to look for in every animal. Avoid buying a horse or pony with bad feet. You will only be buying a load of trouble.

A number of different types of bone are encased inside the hoof, and they all have their own tendons, ligaments and blood vessels. Packed around these bones are layers of sensitive flesh known as laminae, a name you will probably recognise if you

There is always so much to watch at a Show that these spectators are missing a good, clean jump

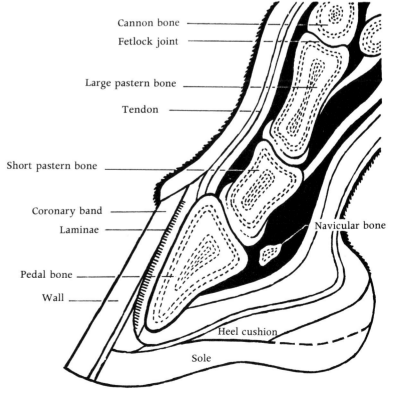

Cannon bone

Fetlock joint

Large pastern bone

Tendon

Short pastern bone

Coronary band

Laminae

Navicular bone

Pedal bone

Wall

Heel cushion

Sole

have ever had a pony with laminitis or fever of the feet. Although the walls and sole of the foot are rigid, the inner structure is able to move because of the rubber-like quality of the frog, that triangular wedge with a cleft in the centre, which is let into the back of the sole and acts as a shock absorber as well as helping the horse to grip. As his foot comes to the ground the frog takes a lot of the weight, in addition to absorbing the concussion. When that happens it depresses, forcing the ends of the walls outwards slightly, and making some movement of the inner structure possible. You can now see why it is so important to clean a horse's feet out regularly and to make sure that stones are not allowed to lodge between the frog and the wall. The frog is also important because it helps pump round the blood to improve the circulation.

Another important part of the hoof is the coronary band which divides the hoof from the skin and hair of the legs, and provides nourishment to the wall, so that it can grow properly. If, for any reason, the coronet becomes damaged, the wall will not grow as it should, and a bulge or split will develop in the crust. Any inflammation of the blood vessels in the foot, either because of poisoning or some other cause, will result in lameness, and the cause of the trouble must be dealt with quickly.

Inflammation is always present in all the injuries and diseases of the feet, and it is important for you to learn to recognise some of the more common. We have already referred to laminitis which is caused when the sensitive laminae, which surrounds the bones of the feet, becomes inflamed. This can be the result of concussion, when the foot hits hard ground, either through too much trotting on the hard road or galloping on rock-hard ground. Most laminitis, however, is caused by incorrect feeding, and occurs in very fat and underworked ponies, usually in the spring and early summer when the grass is particularly lush and rich. It can also occur in stabled horses who do not get enough exercise or horses which are given too much fast work before they are fit.

The disease rarely affects the hind feet, but attacks the front feet so that the animal will become both lame and unwilling to move. To relieve the intense pain in his feet, he will stand with them stuck out in front of his body, with his hind legs drawn forward underneath–rather as though he was leaning with his hindquarters against an imaginary wall. A veterinary surgeon should be sent for promptly–but while you are waiting for him to arrive, the animal's feet should be hosed with cold water and he should be given a bran mash containing about three ounces of Salts.

If the trouble is not dealt with quickly irreparable damage may occur. Once a pony has had an attack of laminitis, care must be taken to see that he does not get another, since after the first he will be particularly susceptible to the disease. You can often see when a pony has had laminitis. The walls of the hoof will have become deformed, due to the bones being forced out of place by the swelling laminae inside the foot. Laminitis is one of the most common of all the foot troubles. It can be cured by rest and careful feeding, but far too many ponies are spoilt because of it.

Far more serious is Navicular disease—which starts with inflammation of the navicular bone situated at the back of the foot, just above the frog. The inflammation can again be caused by too much jumping on hard ground, or by sudden strain. The disease is incurable, although some pain deadening powders can bring temporary relief, because the inflammation will eat into the smooth surface of the navicular bone, roughening it up, so that normal movement of the bone becomes impossible. At first the animal will appear intermittently lame.

Rest will improve the lameness, but the horse will go unsound again as soon as he is put into work. Eventually he becomes permanently lame. Being of an arthritic nature there is no effective cure, although he may be able to remain in work for some time, either by the use of powders, or by an operation known as 'de-ncrving' when the veterinary surgeon cuts the Planta nerve at the back of the leg, making the foot insensible to pain. This will not, however, prevent the disease from developing further, and the operation is never completely satisfactory for this reason.

Some forms of lameness in the foot are fortunately far less serious, and will quickly respond to the correct treatment. Bruising, for example, usually occurs through a horse putting the sole of his foot down hard on a sharp object such as a stone.

He will immediately appear lame, because the bruising will set up inflammation. This can usually be detected. By feeling his feet you will find that the injured foot will appear warmer than the others. The horse will also be unwilling to put any pressure on the foot, and show signs of pain if it is struck lightly with a hammer. The shoe will have to be removed and the injured area poulticed. If it does not respond quickly to treatment a veterinary surgeon should be called.

Other frequent causes of lameness are Corns, caused by shoes pressing into the heels; Sandcracks, splits in the wall of the foot, Thrush, the disease of the frog caused by dirt and neglect, and Seedy-toe—when the sole of the foot separates from the wall, causing the horn to rot inside. Horses also sometimes pick up nails or other pieces of metal. These must be removed as quickly as possible, and the damaged area treated. If any lameness persists for more than a few days, don't hesitate any longer. Get professional advice.

However well your horse or pony is fed and looked after, it will be useless for any real work unless it is shod correctly.

127

Horses have been shod since the times of early civilisation, and over the years a great deal of knowledge has been built up, not only on the action of the foot, but also as to the best forms of shoeing.

Metal shoes have become accepted as the best form of shoe to protect a horse's feet, but in recent years other types of shoes have been tried, including various forms of plastic.

There are two systems of shoeing. Hot shoeing—when the shoe is specially made and tried on hot, so that adjustments can be made before the shoe is finally cooled and nailed on—and cold shoeing—when a ready-made shoe is fitted and altered as far as possible while cold. Hot shoeing is by far the most satisfactory. Whichever system is used there is always one golden rule which should be observed however. The shoe should always be made to fit the foot, and not the foot made to fit the shoe.

Let us look at the six different stages of hot shoeing. To begin with there is the removal, when the blacksmith takes off the old shoe by cutting off all the clenches with his metal 'buffer' and driving hammer, and then levers the shoe off with his 'pincers'. Providing all the clenches have been cut off cleanly, there will be no damage to the wall of the foot when the shoe is removed.

The blacksmith then prepares the foot by cutting away the overgrowth of horn ready for the new shoe to be fitted. Before doing so, however, he must clean out the sole and frog, and make sure that they are both healthy. To cut back the wall he will use either a 'drawing knife', or 'toeing knife', or sometimes a 'horn cutter'. Any ragged parts of the sole or frog will be trimmed as little as possible, and then he will use a 'rasp' to level the foot to give a good bearing surface. If the surface is not level, undue strain will be put on the horse every time his foot touches the ground.

The process of making a new shoe is known as 'forging', and the weight and type of shoe selected will depend either on the nature of the work the horse is expected to do or whether there is any defect in the make-up or action of the horse which needs to be remedied. The solution could be a plain, stamped shoe which consists of an ordinary bar of iron—shaped and stamped with nail holes, and given a toe clip.

He may, however, choose a hunter-shoe made of concave iron, to reduce the risk of it being sucked-off in soft going and additionally to give more grip. If the horse is inclined to 'brush' one leg against another he could use a feather-edged shoe, where the inner part of the shoe has been 'feathered' to fit close in under the wall to reduce the risk of brushing. This type of shoe does not have nail holes along the inner branch.

For a horse or pony being rested at grass he would probably select half length shoes or grass tips to stop the wall of the hoof from splitting at the toe.

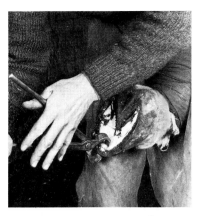  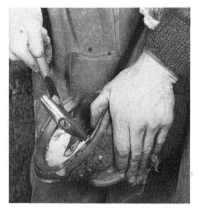

Above, left: preparing the foot;
centre: ensuring a good fit;
right: nailing on the shoe

If he decides on a normal shoe he will shape the iron, and then draw the clips and stamp the nail holes ready for the shoe to be fitted.

This has to be done while it is still hot, and so the blacksmith uses a 'pritchel'–which is a pointed metal tool–to carry the shoe between the horse and his forge. By trying the hot shoe on to the horse's foot he can tell where it sears the horn what adjustments are necessary. When he is satisfied that the shoe is a correct fit it is cooled by being plunged into a bucket of cold water. It is then ready for nailing.

To do this the blacksmith usually starts with the holes at the toe and works round the shoe. The nails used are of a special kind and texture, with heads which have been shaped in such a way that they will always fill the nail hole, even when the shoe is being worn away. The blacksmith is always careful as to how high he drives the nails into the wall of the foot, and as he does so he twists off the sharp end of the nail, leaving a small piece projecting through the wall known as a 'clench'. He then knocks down the clips of the shoe on to the hoof to help hold the shoe in place. He is then ready to tidy up the clenches with his rasp, and make a small groove or 'bed' for them in the wall so they can then be hammered down out of harm's way.

The part where the horn and shoe meet is given a final run round with a rasp, and the toe clip is given a light tap to make sure it is in the correct position. Front shoes usually have one toe clip, and hind shoes have two quarter clips to give greater security.

If the horse is to be used for jumping, the heels may have been provided with additional holes to take heel studs. These are made of special metal in various shapes, and screw into the shoes to give greater grip on take off and landing. They should be removed after the horse has finished jumping, and put away ready for further use.

Frequent shoeing is essential if a horse is to be kept in regular work. This will probably mean a visit from the blacksmith at least once a month. Even ponies turned out for long periods regularly need their feet trimmed.

Screwing in studs to provide a better grip

17
Preparing for competitions

Although many riders get a great deal of pleasure merely from just being on a horse and enjoying the freedom, fresh air and fun that riding has to offer, there are others, with a more competitive nature, who like the additional challenge of riding against other people, and pitting their own skills, and those of their horse, against all comers. Young riders can learn a great deal from taking part in one or more of the equestrian sports, because to do well they and their horses must constantly strive for improvement. They will also develop a clearer insight into the workings of the body and mind of a horse, in order to achieve the mental and physical fitness and condition needed to win.

If you wish to compete you will need knowledge, patience, sympathy, skill as well as a certain amount of nerve, whether you want to Event, Show Jump, compete in Dressage or Show Classes, or just have fun at a local Gymkhana.

There is no quick way to success at anything to do with horses, and competition riding is more time consuming than most. It is the only sport where success lies not just in the performance and ability of the competitor, but in a complete partnership between horse and rider, who must achieve a thorough understanding of each other. Developing this understanding is a fascinating experience, because no two horses are ever really alike, and the creation of a real partnership is not something that can just be learnt merely from a book. Instructors can only lay down guide lines. It must be up to the rider to work out the best way of tackling and overcoming future problems. That is why winning a rosette is something special. It means that horse and rider have had to rely on each other's ability and courage. Neither could have won without the other. This sharing of experiences and opportunities develops character in the rider, and obedience in the horse.

If you decide to compete while you are young, try to take part in as many different types of competition as possible. If you concentrate on just one aspect of riding, you will miss a great deal of fun and experience. You will obviously be limited to some degree by the ability of your horse or pony, unless you are lucky enough to have the chance of riding another horse as well. You

There is always much to be
attended to before having to go
into the ring to be judged

may, however, be very surprised at the willingness and performance of your own animal once you have got him really fit, and properly schooled.

A fit horse needs a fit rider, both mentally and physically.

We will leave it at that, except to say that if you stay up late at a party, and turn up next morning at a show feeling half asleep, do not blame your horse if you make a mess of things. Even if you do not mind, it will not be very fair to an animal, who may have been working hard with you for months trying to get the partnership going.

You may have heard people say that a rider 'had it won before going into the ring'. That is a bit far-fetched, because every horse and rider needs a little luck to win, but it is certainly true that likely victories have been lost before the day either through lack of fitness, lack of schooling, lack of preparation, lack of commonsense, or just lack of care.

Fitness is the first essential. It is ridiculous to ask your horse or pony to compete unless he is feeling fit, and able to exert himself without harm. How would you like to be forced to run a mile at speed when you were unfit? Something would probably go, like a tendon or a blood vessel, which then may take weeks of rest and treatment to repair. The same is true of a horse.

A horse needs time to reach peak fitness, and so your programme of training should start early. It is important to appreciate the difference between 'soft' and 'hard' condition. When a horse is too fat, and has perhaps just come up from grass, with a big round belly, and slack muscles, so that he will sweat and show distress as soon as he is asked to do anything really strenuous, he is said to be in 'soft' condition. He will not be in 'hard' condition until he has got rid of all that superfluous fat, both inside and outside his body, and his muscles and tendons have been toned up to withstand a continuous effort without injury.

Ponies can be particularly deceptive. Although a pony at grass can be perfectly healthy and look fit, his muscles will probably still be soft and flabby, and the space which should be taken up by his lungs will be restricted by his very large stomach, with the result that he will become short of wind when asked to gallop or jump for any length of time.

To sum up: when a horse or pony is in 'hard' condition, the muscles of his limbs will be able to stand up to the strain you are going to impose upon him by hunting, eventing, jumping or some other sport, without causing him to become tired or breakdown. The muscles of the heart will also be equal to the task, and his chest muscles will enable him to breathe fully and easily. His belly must have been slimmed down, so that it will not interfere with the expansion of his lungs.

Providing a horse or pony is sound, only two things will be necessary to make him fit. They are sufficient food, of the right type, and the correct amount of work, again of the right type. As far as food is concerned, we have discussed the rules of feeding and watering, and the various foods needed, in another chapter. Always remember, however, that it will take a horse or pony at least twenty minutes to eat a full corn feed, and one and a half hours in which to digest it. This means that if you are going to work a horse he must be fed at least two hours beforehand. If this is not possible he should only be given a small feed, which can be eaten and digested more quickly. Do not feed too many concentrates to begin with. The amount can be increased as the horse becomes fitter, and the work becomes faster. It also takes a horse or pony about two hours to eat a full hay net, and so let him have his hay after he returns from work. The largest hay net should, of course, always be given at night, when he will have plenty of time to enjoy it and to digest it properly.

When you are getting your animal into hard condition remember that there is also a great deal of difference between 'exercise' and 'work'. When you exercise a horse, you do just enough to keep him fit and well, without asking him for any great exertion. The amount of exercise needed would not necessarily be the same each day, and could range from about twenty minutes, to loosen him up and take any stiffness out of his joints if he has been worked hard the day before, to a good two hours steady exercise. Plenty of fast walking is much better than fast trotting. When you work him, however, you would probably include some schooling and jumping, as well as a certain amount of cantering and galloping. The periods of exercise and work must be co-ordinated if you are to produce a really fit and well trained animal. This will mean weeks and, in some cases, months of steady patient effort.

It is helpful to warn your blacksmith that you are planning to get your horse or pony really fit, because doing so will entail plenty of steady road work. His shoes will not last as long and he will need to be shod more frequently. He may also require a different type of shoe.

As soon as each work period ends, dismount and loosen your horse's girths. Then lead him round until he has cooled-off. Look him over carefully for any knocks or cuts he may have received if you have been galloping or jumping, and feel down his legs for any swellings, because the slow, laborious process of getting an animal really fit and schooled properly will be wasted if he has to be off work through any strains or illness. Always use your own commonsense, and put a horse's welfare and comfort before your own.

Apart from teaching him obedience, you will not really be able to start serious schooling until a horse or pony is able to cope with the extra exertion. When you start schooling remember that you must try and make a horse go forward into every movement,

even when you are teaching him to rein-back. He will need balance and equilibrium in order to carry out each manoeuvre. On your part you must make sure that you are sitting correctly in the centre of the saddle, with your back straight but supple, your hands firm but soft, and your legs kept close to your horse's sides.

If things go wrong, think whether you have been giving the correct signals, and that your horse has been fully aware of exactly what he was expected to do. Say to yourself 'What did I do wrong?' . . . instead of just blaming your horse. When he does something correctly, leave it at that. Make a fuss of him, and move on to something else.

Do not keep on doing the same thing over and over again.

Whatever you are planning to teach him, you must allow time for 'riding-in' before starting work. When you leave the stable let him walk out on a long rein for a few minutes so that he can loosen up, and get used to his surroundings. Then let him go into a nice even trot, making sure that his neck is stretched, and his head is not held too high. His paces should not be too hurried, and you can also let him have a steady canter round the field to take some of the freshness out of him before beginning the lesson.

Before starting, you should already have planned exactly what you intend to do. It is usually a good idea to go over the lesson of the previous day to make sure he has learnt it correctly, before starting something new. Never push a horse too far too fast. It is better to underwork than to overwork him. As soon as he starts to get excited, change to something else until he becomes calm again and is willing to listen and obey your commands. When a horse gets excited his muscles tense up, and his back becomes stiff, so that his movements become jerky and more difficult to control properly.

Never lose your own temper when your horse misbehaves, or you will have lost the day. If you feel that you are losing your self-control, walk your horse round on a long rein. If necessary, take him back to the stable, and try again later.

Whatever branch of equestrian activity you are training for, your horse will have to be supple and obedient, and plenty of flat work is the secret to success. Whether you are going in for dressage, or show jumping, he should be properly collected and balanced, and willing to submit to your demands without question. This will take time and understanding until a real partnership has been built up between you both.

If you are hoping to jump your horse, either in the show ring or across country, you will need to make him active and supple, particularly in the neck, back and loins, and encourage him to jump with boldness and freedom. His balance will have to be flexible enough for him to lengthen or shorten his stride when you tell him, so that his approach to each jump will be correct,

Left: it is important to school a horse on the flat to obtain obedience before asking him to jump

and he will be able to maintain the right amount of impulsion. Apart from the necessary nerve and determination, you must also develop a sense of anticipation, so that you can tell whether his striding is right for him to take off and land correctly.

Most ponies are agile enough to put in a quick stride when they see that they are wrong at a fence, but horses have to be ridden with more precision. That is why it sometimes takes quite a long time for a rider who has been successful jumping ponies to achieve the same amount of success when they start riding horses. For all forms of jumping free forward movement, rhythm and impulsion is essential. A horse should not hold his head too high; a lower head carriage will enable him to round his back more easily, giving him greater freedom of action for his loins and quarters so that he can get greater impulsion.

Checking the foot for risen clenches

Schooling fences should never be too large, but need to be of as much variety as possible. Do not let a horse rush his fences. Circle round until he is ready to listen. If a fence needs to be made larger it is better to increase the spread rather than the height. Finish up by walking a horse quietly among the different jumps on a loose rein, so that he learns not to be bothered by the various shapes, sizes or colours of the fences.

When a horse has learnt to jump single obstacles fluently, and with the necessary degree of obedience, you will have to train him over combination fences of doubles and trebles of the kind to be found in the show jumping ring and on many cross country courses. These provide a test of a horse's jumping ability and training, and the distance between each element will vary according to whether the fences are uprights or spreads. They should be ridden with a straight approach, so that there will be less opportunity for him to run out between fences.

If you have been training a horse or pony with eventing or show jumping in mind, and you feel the time has come to put your schooling and hard work to the test, look for a suitable Show or Event where your animal will be able to compete against other novices, and the fences will not be too large or taxing. Having written away for the entry form, study it carefully to make sure that you and your horse have the necessary qualifications, and that you are fully aware of all the rules and what you will be required to do. Then fill it in and return it along with your entry money. Make a note in your diary of the time, date and venue – it is easy to forget otherwise!

About a week beforehand make a special check of your horse's shoes to make sure that there are no 'risen clenches', that they are not loose, and will be unlikely to give trouble on the day. If you are jumping your horse he will probably require shoes with stud holes, so that you can screw studs in just before you are ready to jump, to give better grip – particularly if the ground is inclined to be rather slippery. Check over all your saddlery to see

Taking off working bandages
before putting on travelling
bandages

that it is in good order, and that you are not planning to use any item which may not be allowed by the judges.

The day before you are due to compete, give your horse some gentle exercise, and an extra thorough grooming. Then clean your tack carefully, and put ready all the equipment you will need for yourself and your horse. Cross-country courses can also usually be walked the day before the event, but show jumping courses have to be walked on the day, in the time allotted by the judges before the start of a class. Remember to get to bed early, but before you do so, take a final look at your horse or pony to make sure that he is comfortable, and has everything he wants.

On the day, be up in plenty of time so that you will not have

This home-made practice jump,
with a brightly coloured pole, is
serving its purpose

A practice cross-country obstacle
can be built at the side of a field
by using brush and rustic poles

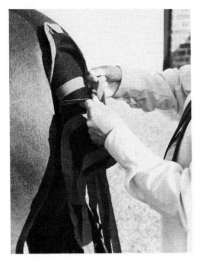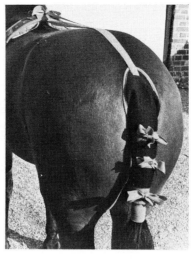

Putting on a tail guard to give protection when travelling

to rush, and give yourself time in which to deal with any last minute problems. If the Show or Event is some distance from home, and you are going to have to travel by horsebox, bandage your horse carefully. In addition to his tack, make sure you put on board your stick, an extra head collar and rope, an anti-sweat rug; hay net, and a small feed (if he is going to be away all day), a water bucket (and supply of fresh water), and a first aid kit (in case you have to deal with any cuts or bruises). You will probably prefer to change into your riding clothes when you get to the show providing there is time, but you might also take with you an extra pair of jodhpurs or breeches in case your others get split. You will also need a macintosh in the event of rain, and a pair of rubber boots, if the ground looks like being wet or muddy.

No doubt you already made sure that your horse was easy to box before buying him, but if you had not already done so, do not leave it until the day to find out!

Load him quietly in the box and tie him securely, so that he has enough room in which to move his head about freely, and steady his legs against the motion of the box when it is cornering or moving across rough ground. Always leave home with plenty of time in hand so that the journey does not have to be rushed and you can arrive at the ground a good hour or so before your own particular event or class is scheduled to start. When you arrive, and your box has been parked safely, make sure that your horse is all right, and either leave him in the box, or tie him up to the side, before going off to the secretary's office to check numbers and see that your entry is correct. Find out where the collecting ring is, and be certain you know exactly where you should be . . . and at what time.

Horses and ponies vary in the amount of 'riding-in' they require before a class, but allow yourself plenty of time to see that he is saddled and bridled correctly and that you have an

Competitors checking the order of jumping at the collecting ring

opportunity of warming him up properly before he is asked to jump. There will usually be a practice jump available. This need not be particularly high. It is there to help you to loosen him up and get him jumping accurately, rather than to find out whether he can jump high enough. You should have found that out before you entered him!

If you are show jumping, listen for the loudspeaker announcement telling you when you can walk the course. Do this carefully—working out your line or track and checking the distances between the fences. Then when you have found out the order of jumping, see that you report to the collecting ring steward in plenty of time. While you are waiting your turn do not gallop about the ground. You will be a nuisance to spectators and other competitors and you will only be tiring your horse unnecessarily and probably be getting him too excited.

After you have finished, and he has done his best, make a fuss of him and get off and loosen his girths. Then walk him round until he is cool. Let him have a mouthful or two of water when you return to the horsebox. If you have another class later in the day, and you decide to give him a feed, make sure you leave plenty of time for him to digest it.

At the end of the day bandage him up again carefully, and check that he has his hay net, and is comfortable in the horsebox before setting off on the journey home.

Clothes to be worn will depend on what you are doing. Some types of competition or sport require special clothing, but whether you are show jumping, eventing, or even playing polo, there are four golden rules which must be observed. Always wear a hard hat; always wear the correct dress; always make sure that you are neat and tidy, and always observe the competition or other rules.

Glossary

ADJUSTABLE HEAD COLLAR a head collar which has an adjustable head strap, noseband and throat strap.

AGAINST THE CLOCK a term used in show jumping when competitors 'jump off', and where, in the event of equality of faults, time decides the result.

AGED when a horse is seven years old or more.

AIDS the signals given to a horse by a rider to convey his wishes, or the means by which the signals are produced.

ANTICAST ROLLER or ARCH ROLLER a type of stable roller which has a metal arch to prevent the horse from rolling over in his box.

APRON-FACED a horse which has a large white mark on his face.

ARCH-MOUTH PELHAM a pelham bit which has a mouthpiece with an upward curve.

ARTZEL a white mark on the forehead of a horse.

ATHERSTONE GIRTH usually made of baghide leather and shaped to give extra movement at the horse's elbows to prevent any chafing.

BANDAGES protective strips of material used on the legs and the tail mainly as a protection.

BANBURY MOUTHPIECE a mouthpiece of a bit which has a rounded bar which is tapered in the centre and fitted into slots in the cheekpieces.

BARREL a horseshoe which has a metal piece welded across the heel to give additional support. By placing additional pressure on the horse's frog it can provide relief if a horse has corns or sidebones.

BED DOWN to make a bed for a horse.

BEHIND THE BIT when a horse refuses to take a proper hold of his bit.

BIB MARTINGALE a running Martingale with a triangular leather centrepiece.

BITLESS BRIDLE a bridle without a bit which acts on the chin and nose carriage.

BLAIR BRIDLE a type of bitless bridle with long cheekpieces.

BLAZE a white marking on a horse extending the full length of the face.

BLEMISH any scar left by an injury or wound which does not affect a horse's performance or health.

BLOOD HORSE an English Thorough-bred.

BLOOM the gloss or shine on a horse's coat.

BOBTAILED a horse with a very short docked tail.

BOG SPAVIN a soft non-painful swelling on the inside and slightly to the front of the hock joint.

BONE SPAVIN a hard bony swelling on the inside lower edge of the hock joint.

BOOT HOOK metal hooks which pass through the webbing loops on the inside of riding boots to help pull them on.

BORE when a horse leans on the bit.

BREAK OUT when a horse sweats suddenly.

BREASTPLATE a wide strap attached to the saddle to keep it from sliding back on the horse (sometimes called a Breast Girth).

BRUSHING the act of a horse striking the inside of one leg near the fetlock joint, with the opposite hoof or shoe (also known as cutting).

BRUSHING BOOTS usually made of leather or felt with a padded portion running down the inside to give protection to the joints if a horse strokes one leg against another.

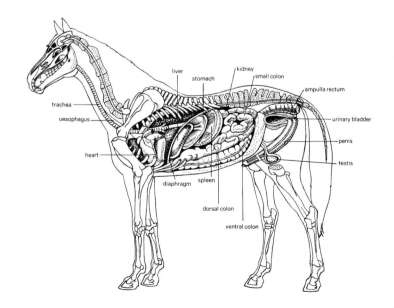

CADE FOAL a foal reared by hand.

CAMP when a horse stands with his fore and hind legs spread as far apart as possible.

CANKER a morbid growth of the horn on the foot.

CANNON BONE the solid bone between the knee and the fetlock of a horse. It should be short for strength and look flat from the side.

CAPPED HOCK a swelling on the joint of the hock usually caused through shortage of bedding or when a horse is travelling.

CAST when a horse loses a shoe; when hounds attempt to regain the scent of their quarry at a check, or when a horse lies down in his box and is unable to get up usually because of an obstruction in the box.

CHANGE LEADS when a horse changes the leading leg when cantering or galloping.

CHANGE OF LEG a movement in cantering when a horse is made to lead with the other leg.

CINCH UP an American term for fastening the girth of a horse.

CLENCH the pointed end of a nail which protrudes through the hoof after a horse has been shod (sometimes called a Clinch).

COAT CASTING horses cast their coats twice a year.

COLIC pain in the digestive organs of a horse.

COLLECTED TROT a slow controlled trot.

COLLECTED WALK a slow walk in which the horse moves resolutely forward.

COLT an ungelded male horse less than four years old.

CONDITION the term used for the looks and health of a horse.

CONTACT the link which the hands of a rider have with a horse's mouth through the reins.

COW HOCKS hocks which turn inwards.

CRACKED HEELS inflammation of the skin in the hollow of the horse's heel.

CREST the ridge along the back of a horse's neck where the mane grows.

CRIB BITING a bad vice in horses where a horse bites his crib or some other protection and at the same time swallows air. This habit is frequently started by boredom and is usually associated with wind-sucking.

CUP the metal holder which fits onto the wing of a show jump to hold the pole in position.

DRESSAGE a series of exercises to show a horse's obedience to his rider's commands.

DROPPED NOSE-BAND a nose band sometimes used with a snaffle bit to prevent a horse from opening his mouth too wide or allowing the bit to slide to one side.

DROPPINGS a horse's dung.

ELECTUARY the term used for a medicine for horses in which the drugs are made into a paste with a base of treacle or honey.

FODDER a word used to describe any foodstuff normally fed to horses (sometimes called Forage).

FORGING when the hind shoe of a horse strikes the fore shoe, usually at a trot. This usually occurs when the animal is being allowed to trot in an uncollected or slovenly manner. The term can also refer to the making of a horse shoe.

FROG the V-shaped formation in the sole of a horse's foot.

FROG-CLEFT the natural depression in the centre of the frog at the widest part.

FRONT the term to indicate the part of the horse which is in front of the rider in the saddle.

FULL-MOUTH a horse at six years old.

FULLERING a groove in the ground surface of a horse shoe in which the nail holes are placed.

FULMER SNAFFLE a cheek snaffle fitted with a broad jointed mouth-piece and loose rings (sometimes called an Australian Horse Ring Snaffle).

GALL a sore place caused by badly fitting saddlery, usually found under the girth of a saddle particularly when a horse is in soft condition.

GIRTH SLEEVE a sleeve of sheepskin or rubber which passes over the girth to prevent galling.

GIVE WITH THE HAND opening the fingers sufficiently to relax the tension of the reins.

GONE IN THE WIND a term applied to any affection of a horse's wind, and indicates that the horse is of 'unsound wind'.

GOOSE RUMPED when the slope of a horse's quarters runs acutely from the highest point to the root of the tail (sometimes called Drooping Quarters).

HALF PASS when the horse goes diagonally forward and sideways on two tracks, the forehand leading the quarters, and the head flexed in the direction of movement.

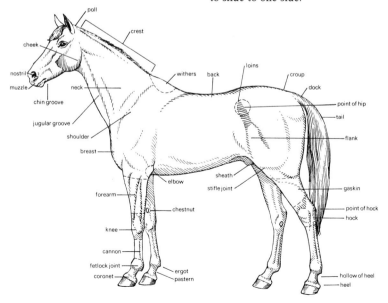

poll
crest
cheek
nostril
muzzle
neck
chin groove
jugular groove
shoulder
breast
forearm
chestnut
knee
cannon
fetlock joint
coronet
ergot
pastern
elbow
withers
back
loins
croup
dock
point of hip
tail
flank
sheath
stifle joint
gaskin
point of hock
hock
hollow of heel
heel

HAM-STRING the tendon that runs down the behind part of the second thigh to the point of the hock.

HAND the measurement by which the height of a horse or pony is calculated – 10 cm (4 inches).

HOGGING a term used for removing the mane.

HORSE BLANKET a thick blanket used under a night rug in cold weather.

KNEE-CAPS a felt covering to protect the horse's knees during working exercise or when travelling.

KNEE SPAVIN a bony growth at the back of the knee.

LAMINITIS inflamation or fever of the feet, usually caused by fast work on hard ground or too much rich grass or heating food without enough exercise.

LIP STRAP a thin leather strap which holds the curb chain in place.

MUCKING OUT the process of cleaning a horse box or stall and removing the droppings.

MUCK HEAP the name frequently given to a manure heap.

MUD FEVER inflamation of the heels, legs or belly.

NAVICULAR a disease of the navicular bone, usually confined to the forefeet.

OVER-REACH BOOT a circular rubber boot used to prevent injury to the coronet when a horse over-reaches.

OVER-REACHING when the toe of the hind shoe strikes against the heel of the forefeet.

PADDOCK an enclosed area of grassland used for grazing horses or ponies.

PINCERS an instrument used by a blacksmith.

PLAITING the process of putting plaits into a horse's mane or tail to improve the appearance.

PRITCHEL a pointed metal tool used by a blacksmith to carry a hot shoe.

PULLED MANE OR TAIL when the hair from the underneath of the mane or side of the dock is removed by pulling to give a tidy effect.

PULSE a horse's pulse is normally 36 to 40 beats to the minute. It is usually taken at the submaxillary artery under the jaw.

ROLLER a form of girth made of leather, webbing or hemp to keep a rug in place.

RUGGING UP a term used for putting rugs on a horse.

SADDLE-HORSE a wooden stand upon which saddles can be placed for cleaning or storage.

SADDLE SOAP a specially prepared soap which is applied with a damp sponge for cleaning saddles, bridles and other leather harness.

SIDE BONE a hard lump on the coronet on either side of the heel.

SIDE REINS reins attached to the roller for training purposes or when lunging a young horse.

SIDE SADDLE a saddle, usually used by women, when the rider sits sideways on a horse.

SKIP a wicker-type basket or metal container used to collect droppings in a stable.

SPLINT a small bony growth between the splint bone and the cannon bone.

STALL a compartment for a horse in a stable in which a horse must be tied.

SWEET ITCH an irritable condition of the skin at the crest, withers and croup in summer.

TACK the name given to describe the saddlery used on a horse or pony.

TEMPERATURE the normal temperature of a horse is 38°C (100·5°F).

TENDON BOOTS specially designed boots, usually of leather, which protect the tendons.

TENDONS Fibrous structures forming bands and cords attaching the muscles to the bones of the legs.

TRIMMING tidying the hairs of a horse's head, mane and tail.

WARBLES lumps in the region of the saddle caused by the warble fly.

WITHER PAD a pad made of soft material placed under the saddle to prevent undue pressure on a horse's back, particularly when the saddle does not fit well.

WOLF TEETH rudimentary teeth in front of the upper and lower molar teeth.

WORMS parasites which can affect the condition of a horse.

Acknowledgements

Action Photography 106, 121; John Elliot 10, 14, 17T, 21T, 25, 26, 27L, 33, 35, 107, 131; Equestrian (Press & General) Services Limited 12, 13, 15, 16, 17B, 18, 27, 39, 40, 42, 43, 45, 46, 47, 49, 51, 52, 53, 54, 55, 57, 58, 59, 60, 61, 63, 64, 65, 66, 67, 70, 72, 74, 76, 77, 78, 80, 81, 83, 84, 85, 86, 87, 88, 89, 91, 92, 93, 95, 96, 97, 99, 101, 103, 107, 108, 109, 111, 112, 117, 118, 119, 120, 126, 127, 129, 131, 134, 136, 137, 138, 139, 140, 141; Leslie Lane 21B, 24, 25, 26TB, 28, 29, 31, 36, 37; Sally Anne Thompson 22, Tony Stone Associates 23. Hamlyn Group Picture Library front jacket; British Tourist Authority back jacket.